Puskas on Puskas

Puskas on Puskas

The life and times of a footballing legend

Edited and translated by
Rogan Taylor and Klara Jamrich

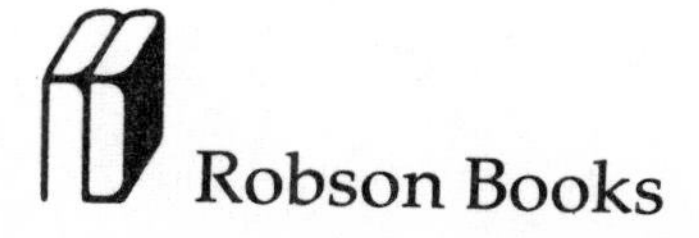

First published in Great Britain in 1997 by Robson Books Ltd, Bolsover House, 5–6 Clipstone Street, London W1P 8LE

Extracts from *Oromok es Csalodasok* is reproduced by kind permission of Erzebet Sebes.

British Library Cataloguing in Publication Data
A catalogue record for this title is available from the British Library

ISBN 1 86105 083 6

Photoset in North Wales in Plantin by Derek Doyle & Associates, Mold, Flintshire. Printed and bound in Great Britain by Butler & Tanner Ltd, London and Frome.

To the Stalinist Evertonian
who told me the Hungarians were coming
and for my dad who bought the telly.

'But yet to come were the men who surpassed them all, the team which for romance, for fierceness of purpose, for rhythm in motion, for beauty in action, for fire, and fury and elegance and bubbling personality was perhaps the greatest football team there ever was – the men from the Danube . . . and, above all, the *élan* of Puskas, the vibrant, vibrating personality of Puskas in possession of the ball, the arrogance of his shooting, the superiority of his playing mannerisms.'

(Bob Ferrier, *Soccer Partnership*, London, 1960)

Contents

Acknowledgements

The primary acknowledgement must go to the subject of this book, Ferenc Puskas, who willingly agreed to support the project and gave generously of his time to enable it to be accomplished.

We must thank, too, all the others who consented to be interviewed, some repeatedly, about their memories of Puskas. We are grateful for their patience and understanding. We would also like formally to recognize the significance of the BBC TV series *Kicking and Screaming*, and its producer Jean-Claude Bragard, in not only providing the initial opportunity to conduct research interviews with all the surviving players from the Hungarian Golden Squad, but also for the use of appropriate extracts from some of the interviews made during that research. Thanks, too, to Brian Barwick at BBC Sport for allowing us the privilege of looking after the 'great man' before his appearance on *Sports Review of the Year* (1993).

There are a number of other people who have helped considerably, either with advice, readings of the manuscript, practical assistance or simple encouragement. These include: Tim Dawson, Sam Johnstone, Peter Law, Ray Spiller, Nigel

Swain, Nora Samogyi, Valeria Toth, Andrew Ward, John Williams and Jim Woolridge.

Finally, Rogan Taylor would like to express his appreciation of the time and support made available by the University of Liverpool, especially the staff of the Department of Social and Economic History, without which the completion of this book would have been impossible.

Rogan Taylor and Klara Jamrich,
Liverpool and Budapest, 1997

Introduction

The man

Ferenc Puskas is one of the greatest players of the century and the most prolific international goalscorer of all time. For some people, perhaps especially in Hungary, he was – and he remains – the greatest footballer of them all. But regardless of precisely where in football's hierarchy Puskas should properly be lodged, there can be no doubt that it is in the same chamber as Pele, Di Stefano, Best, Cruyff, Maradona and the other recognized gods of the game.

It is surprising, therefore, to find that apart from one semi-ghosted autobiography, *Captain of Hungary* (Cassell, London, 1955), there is no full account in English of Puskas's life and times. This seems even more remarkable when one discovers what an amazing life it was, lived through such dramatic times. No one in football's pantheon has a tale to tell quite like Puskas has.

As a player, he led two distinct, consecutive – and stunning – footballing lives, either one of which would have been enough to qualify him for a place amongst the elite of the game. His first, as captain of Kispest/Honved and Hungary, collapsed after his refusal to return to Budapest following the great Uprising in October 1956, which was crushed by Soviet tanks within days of its birth. From spring 1950 to February 1956, the Hungarian national team under Puskas's leadership had lost only one match: the World Cup Final of 1954. They had beaten Italy in Rome, 3–0; England at Wembley, 6–3 (in Budapest, 7–1); Uruguay and Brazil, both 4–2 and Germany, 8–3. The tactical innovations introduced to the world by the Hungarian's in that period led directly to the development of the 4–2–4 system (which Hungarian coaches like Bela Guttmann took to Brazil), and the positional fluidity that was encouraged amongst the players produced the modern prototype of 'total football'.

By October 1956, Puskas was almost thirty with, apparently, his best days behind him. His refusal to return home after the Uprising brought him a one-year ban from the Hungarian FA, converted by FIFA into an eighteen-month, worldwide ban. Long after fellow defectors Czibor and Kocsis had been snapped up by Barcelona, Puskas languished in Italy. He could neither train nor play in any professional environment. He became depressed; his weight ballooned; his career was over. What happened next? Puskas served the ban, signed for Real Madrid at the height of the club's powers and played for almost a decade in Spain, winning five league championships along the way.

It seems more than the life of just one great footballer. Yet Puskas played for only three teams over a twenty-three-year career – Kispest/Honved, Hungary and Real Madrid.* During his periods with these teams, they were arguably the best football sides in the world. Though he played nearly all his football in the top flight of his profession, he was never bought or sold in his life. In the Hungarian national team during the first half of the 1950s, he also presided over such a flowering of tactical richness, skill and imagination that it amounted to a virtual re-invention of the game itself.

* This is ignoring his four caps for Spain.

Puskas was amazingly prolific. He scored over 250 league goals for each of the two clubs he played for, and his international and European goalscoring record – 83 in 84 matches for Hungary; 35 in 37 for Real in European competitions – makes (to use British examples) Bobby Charlton and Ian Rush look like also-rans. Even Pele could only manage 76 goals for Brazil in a career spanning four World Cups (of which his team won three). Yet Puskas – who played for Hungary in but one World Cup (and then only in three matches due to injury) and left his national team prematurely, aged twenty-nine – still holds the all-time international goalscoring record. In all probability, it will never be surpassed.

To cap it all, Puskas played in two of the most historically significant – not to mention wonderful – football matches of modern times: England v Hungary at Wembley in 1953, and Real Madrid v Eintracht Frankfurt at Hampden Park in 1960. Surely enough for two lives at least?

The times

During the first of his footballing lives, Puskas lived through some of the most dramatic and turbulent times in Hungary's history. His professional career began at the age of sixteen with Kispest Football Club in 1943, in a Budapest still largely untouched by the war, despite the Hungarian government's alliance with Nazi Germany. Within six years, he witnessed the bloody conclusion of the war (as the Russians fought the Germans street by street through the capital for two months), the liberation of his country and a brief budding of democracy; followed by a seven-year reign of one of the most rigorously Stalinistic regimes in the whole of Eastern Europe. Mass imprisonments, forced deportations, labour camps, show trials, torture, summary executions – the full panoply of the tools of tyranny was in use until, and even beyond, the Hungarian Uprising of 1956.

Yet in the midst of this massively restrictive society, one great freedom miraculously flourished. On a patch of green grass, the Hungarian national football players and their coaches redefined the game that the English had codified almost a century before them. With a core of half-a-dozen immensely talented and tactically astute players – Grosics, Hidegkuti, Bozsik, Kocsis, Czibor and Puskas – a virtually unbeatable team was assembled that took on all-comers for six glorious years of international competition. Tom Finney still describes them as 'the finest footballing side' he ever encountered and, for many, they remain the best national team ever to play the game. In Hungary today, they are still known simply as the Golden Squad.

Puskas was the golden boy at the heart of the Golden Squad. Yet he hardly looked the part. He was short and squat, liked to eat more than he should, was almost totally one-footed and rarely deigned to head the ball. But his strength in possession, that peerless left foot, the cannonball shot and a brilliant tactical brain made his football sparkle like a firework.

The politics

As Puskas and the others – like his quiet colleague and childhood friend at Kispest, the wing-half Jozsef Bozsik – were forged into an invincible team, the Hungarian political regime recognized in them one of the most potent propaganda tools for socialism that they could wish for. From 1950–54, the unbeaten national team was frequently paraded at great state occasions and Party gatherings as evidence of the success of the Hungarian system. Puskas –

the poor kid from Kispest – was living proof of the genius dormant in the proletariat, a genius only liberated through socialism. He was the exemplary diamond – and a rough one, too – glinting amongst the unconsidered masses.

For a few years, in the midst of this model, Stalinistic society, Puskas – almost alone outside senior political circles – was virtually *unassailable*. In fact, given the procession of show trials which threatened even the most elevated of Hungarian politicians, the national football captain enjoyed greater personal security than many of the most powerful men leading the country. But if Puskas was the golden boy of the communist regime, ironically he was also the darling of the would-be entrepreneurs and street-wise capitalists who saw him as a 'smart operator', smuggling in more nylons and watches than anyone else when the victorious team returned from their travels abroad, past acquiescent customs officers at the Hungarian border.

Puskas was not slow to realize, and exploit, his unique situation. From childhood, he seems to have possessed inherent cunning, cleverness and a wayward, spontaneous streak, indulged (perhaps over-indulged) on the football pitch by a succession of trainers and coaches, including his father, who were probably in awe of his talent and confidence. Even as a sixteen-year-old for Kispest, his voice was often the loudest on the park, issuing a stream of instructions and criticisms directed sometimes at players many years his senior. There were some who railed at such outrageous cheek, but he performed on the pitch and became an undisputedly great player, so who could argue with him?

Puskas was courted by powerful men within the regime but he was also the favourite of the dispossessed and the powerless. He was known affectionately in Hungary – as he still is today – by his childhood nickname, 'Ocsi' (pronounced 'Urtchie'), which means 'kid brother'. But it was his uncultured, ribald and unbowed attitude to those in positions of great power that brought him a place in the hearts of the have-nots and the wannabees. For a start, Puskas could 'fix' almost anything, his connections were so good, and he gave help to many who asked for it.

Stories of Puskas's disrespect for authority regularly circulated in Budapest and he was greatly admired for it. He tweaked the noses of the mighty, many of whom liked and admired him despite his unruliness. One player who was a colleague in the national team recalls Puskas fooling around with one of the most feared politicians of his time, Mihaly Farkas, Minister of Defence and informally responsible for the hated security police, the AVH. Farkas was visiting the team one day at the prestigious army facilities on Margaret Island, wearing an all-white military uniform. Puskas collapsed with laughter when he saw him: 'I thought you were the ice-cream boy, at last,' he told the man whose son was one of the regime's leading torturers. The room went quiet as everyone waited to see Farkas's reaction. Could even Puskas get away with this?

But what could Farkas have done? Not only did Puskas's Hungarian team carry all before them on the football pitch, but they also did it with a style and, for the politically attuned, with an ideological purity that was invaluable to the regime. For the tactical innovations wrought by the Hungarians were seen in some circles (by no means confined to either Hungary or the Soviet bloc) as a political metaphor. This was 'socialist' football, played by a world-class team led by a working-class genius. Even Puskas – as unpolitical, non-ideological a person as one could meet in real life – used phrases like 'sharing the work out equally' to describe elements of the tactical reorganization of the team that constituted part of their football 'revolution'. Of course, few players saw it as a political game (though they were naturally aware of the political credibility their success bestowed on the regime). But one man almost certainly did recognize the ideological dimensions of the tactical innovations: Gusztav Sebes, the national coach of the Hungarian team throughout its greatest period, and a major contributor to the innovations himself.

The coach

Sebes was a 'good communist' with an appropriate track record that included organizing the Renault car workers of Paris in the 1930s. When he became Hungary's national coach after the war, he saw at once the advantages that a highly centralized, command-control system of administration might confer on football. (It was a model, of course, already in use in Soviet football.) Sebes could, for example, corral almost his entire national team in one club side and keep most of his reserves in another, playing the same tactical system week by week. Having the ear of the most powerful politicians, he could prepare for particular international games by arranging special matches against other club teams, directing their tactics to imitate the coming opponents, just as he did before the famous encounter with England at Wembley in 1953.

Sebes could experiment with the national team players – and their tactics – in quiet, mid-week matches outside the capital, on a regular basis without risk. He could even conscript young players he wanted into his core-club, Kispest, which was soon renamed Honved, 'the defenders of the homeland' club, representing the Hungarian army. All the club's players were, nominally, in the army and therefore officially 'amateurs', though they lived and trained as professionals. Yet despite all his power, Sebes was wise enough not to force a rigid tactical system on his gifted players; instead he encouraged an atmosphere that allowed maximum freedom to the great individual talents that history had bequeathed him. Nevertheless, the ensemble was undoubtedly a team.

The Hungarian Uprising and its aftermath melted down the Golden Squad that Sebes had assembled, and three of its key members, Kocsis, Czibor and Puskas, never again played for their national team after 1956 (though Puskas turned out three times for Spain in the 1962 World Cup). When he arrived in Madrid in 1958, two stones overweight and the wrong side of thirty, Puskas looked an enormous gamble for Real's owner Santiago Bernabeu. Even more unpredictable was the possible reaction of the club's greatest star and leading goalscorer, Alfredo Di Stefano from Argentina, for many the best centre-forward in the world at the time (and a candidate for the greatest of all time), and someone quite capable of seeing off any imported star he failed to get on with, as the brilliant Brazilian, Didi, discovered to his cost. It was during this crucial period in Puskas's life, his first twelve months with Real Madrid in 1958–59, that he drew in full measure on all his determination and discipline – often under-rated by those who did not know him well – which would be essential for him to succeed in difficult, even hostile circumstances.

The challenge

Puskas was ridiculed at first by Real's fans (and probably some team-mates) when they saw the pot-belly and apparent lack of pace. The Real coach, Carniglia, didn't want him either. But Puskas lost the extra weight in a few months and was soon scoring as frequently as Di Stefano himself. As his first season in Spain reached a climax, the two great players were neck-and-neck, equal top goalscorers in the Spanish first division. But Puskas was wise enough to know that he needed the friendship and support of the temperamental Argentinian. Towards the end of the last match of the season, Puskas laid off a ball for Di Stefano to score, rather than taking the goal himself.

Puskas went on to forge a wonderful partnership with Di

Stefano which brought a string of championships with Real Madrid and even greater glory in the European Cup. He retired as a player in 1967 and began a peripatetic career as a coach that would take him from Paraguay to Australia, and many stations between. But not to Hungary. Puskas remained for nearly a quarter of a century in exile from his native land; an exile largely self-imposed towards the end, one that perhaps reflected the painful memories of his treatment in Budapest after the Hungarians had failed to win the 1954 World Cup, and the Hungarian FA's ban imposed on him after 1956.

He refused to return home – not even for the funeral of his life-long friend Bozsik – until twenty-five years after his departure. Even then, in 1981, it required a determined posse, including Sebes, Puskas's wife Erzebet, senior politicians and a famous Hungarian film director, to persuade him to return to Hungary to take part in a reunion of the Golden Squad and a film project about the team. He was received on his return like a long-lost national hero, though it was another eleven years before he took up permanent residence in Budapest, where he lives today.

A Personal Prologue

The sensitive reader will have already realized that I am a Puskas fan. It was the headmaster of my junior school in Liverpool who unwittingly facilitated it. At lunch-time on 25 November 1953, he shut the school and sent us all home (those were the days) to witness the afternoon friendly match billed as 'the world championship decider': England, undefeated at home by continental opposition since 1066, versus Hungary, Olympic champions and unbeaten for three years. Consequently, I first became aware of Puskas and the rest of that wonderful Hungarian team as an impressionable eight-year-old, watching the match on a tiny television set my family had only just acquired. In fact, I am for ever in debt to the Hungarians in general – and of course to Puskas in particular – for their unknowing bequest to me of a passion for football; gorgeous, glorious, victorious football. I had no idea how it would shape my life in the end.

It was Puskas who first indelibly illustrated what it was to play the game properly, with touch, imagination and outlandish spontaneity. I literally fell in love with the game there and then. I saw the point of it all for the first time. Maybe I would have fallen for football anyway. But Hungary were my primary team (and later Real Madrid too, because *he* played for them) though I eventually deigned to watch, and finally support wholeheartedly, a local outfit, Liverpool FC, just after a chap called Bill Shankly came along to manage them. But first love is always and for ever first love, isn't it?

I had a 'political' introduction to the match, too. My best friend was the eldest son of a communist family in Liverpool, and it was he who informed me, long before the match itself, that we were going to witness 'socialist football' in its prime – the team game that would brush aside a collection of individuals, even if the latter did include Englishmen of the calibre of Stanley Matthews, Stan Mortensen, Tom Finney and Billy Wright (though in the end, Finney didn't play).

After the match – a magnificent 6–3 victory for the Hungarians – we were convinced. Socialist football was the future. Who could fail to read the writing on the wall? Even long after the Wembley game lost its political hue – and the brutal repression of the Hungarian Uprising expunged any superficial ideological message – the real significance of the match remained. Football could be a wondrous thing, an object worthy of a lifetime's devotion; a vision of joy and of perfection too.

The book

Many years after that historic match, I found myself becoming involved with football not just as a fan but as a writer and broadcaster. In 1993, I became a consultant for a six-part series for BBC TV – *Kicking and Screaming* – recording the social history of football in England since the turn of the century. I travelled to Budapest to meet Puskas and research the Wembley game (someone had to do it), and a few months later returned with producer and crew to film interviews with players and others who remembered the occasion. As it happened, we were in Budapest on 25 November that year – the anniversary of England's defeat by the Hungarians – and in the evening we filmed a huge celebration dinner to which all the surviving players who took part were invited. It was there that I found myself – forty years to the very day since I watched that match – briefly at a table with Puskas, Hidegkuti, Grosics, Buzanszky and Czibor; George Robb, Jackie Sewell and Sir Stanley Matthews.

Puskas flew to London a few weeks later to be the special guest of honour on the BBC's *Sports Review of the Year*. During his stay, I suggested to Klara Jamrich – the Hungarian researcher/interpreter for the television programme, who had accompanied him – that we jointly propose a book to Puskas. To our delight, he agreed to co-operate, and in Budapest during part of September 1994 and again in 1995, he made himself available to us every morning for a series of lengthy recorded interviews about his life.

What follows is the result of those interviews, an oral history of his life largely in the words of Puskas himself, translated into English by Klara Jamrich, edited and re-polished by me. I have also included, where appropriate, brief historical sketches of the political developments in Hungary which ran parallel to Puskas's career in his own country. In addition, further interviews were conducted with contemporary players and commentators, and written sources, some previously unavailable in English, were researched and translated by Klara Jamrich and subsequently interwoven into the text by me.

So here it is, a labour of love: the life and times of Ferenc Puskas, one of the most remarkable and talented of footballers, and for me personally an *initiator* into the joyous magic of the game. Puskas celebrates his seventieth birthday in April 1997. As he looks back across a career that spans over half a century as player, coach and manager, he exudes a deep sense of satisfaction to be back home in Budapest after so many years of exile. These days he is still a regular at Kispest where his career first began, and he remains in an advisory role to the Hungarian FA. He keeps close to the game indeed, as I discovered, his life has been soaked in football, from his earliest moments of consciousness . . .

Rogan Taylor

1

Childhood to 1946

'If you kick with both feet, you fall on your arse.'

The defeat of Germany in 1918 brought the collapse of the Hapsburg Empire, within which Hungary had been a junior partner with Austria. In November that year Hungary declared itself a republic, but the government fell the following year and the Hungarian Soviet Republic – a coalition of communists and social democrats – briefly appeared in 1919, only to fall a few months later to counter-revolutionary forces headed by the powerful leadership of Admiral Miklos Horthy. The right-wing, nationalist regime led by Horthy ruled Hungary until the end of the Second World War.

Puskas: I was born in April 1927 in Kispest, which was then on the very outskirts of Budapest. It was only a village really, with very modest dwellings. My family lived in a small flat in the so-called 'town houses' that were newly built, three or four storeys high, right next to Kispest Football Club. One of my earliest memories is the roar of the crowd through our kitchen window on match days. It fascinated me.

The surrounding streets teemed with kids. Everyone was

quite poor and few could buy toys, but football provided us with enormous, cheap fun. Some of my relatives insist that I first kicked a ball when I was only nine or ten months old, and only just standing up. Even as a three-year-old, I could run well enough to keep up with a game.

We street kids often spent every waking hour together; we grew up together and some of us went on to become life-long friends. Football was our passion. My sister Eva often wanted to join us but girls were not allowed to play, so I would send her home to fetch me a slice of bread and dripping. We didn't have a decent pitch to play on, of course, but there were lots of vacant building sites, *grunds* as we called them, all over Budapest, with kids playing football on them. We didn't always have boots to play in, especially in the early days, so we played barefoot on any sandy patch we could find.

Often we had no real ball to play with either, so someone would make a rag ball or steal a tennis ball from somewhere. It was anything we could get, really. We formed teams and played boys from other streets, and these could turn into quite serious matches. Sometimes, on big occasions, we would nick a real ball from the football club and return it quietly afterwards. That was only possible because my father became a player at Kispest.

Puskas's father first played for Kispest in 1927 when the family name was 'Purczeld', a surname that reflected the German origins of Puskas's ancestors. As nationalism increased under the Horthy regime during the 1930s, Hungarians with foreign-sounding names came under increasing pressure from local authorities and employers to change their names and, around 1935, the Purczeld family altered their name to 'Puskas'. Not to have done so would have been a political statement of German sympathies.

Ocsi

Ferenc Puskas is known to almost everyone in Hungary as 'Ocsi', which means 'kid brother'. Even his wife calls him by this nickname. (Today, as a term of respect, the word 'Bacsi', which means 'Uncle' is often added so it becomes 'Ocsi Bacsi': 'uncle kid brother'.) He first received the nickname as a child, according to Gyorgy Szepesi, the leading football commentator in Hungary, who first saw Ocsi play in 1942 in a youth cup final against Ferencvaros.

Szepesi: There is a story about how Ocsi got his nickname. He was ill with a cold and ordered to stay at home in bed while his father went training at Kispest and his mother went shopping. He escaped through a window and joined his mates playing football on some waste ground. But his mother spotted him on her way home and got the rolling-pin to threaten him, determined to give him a good hiding. When she arrived, the other kids surrounded Puskas to protect him, saying, 'Don't beat him, Mrs Puskas, he's our kid brother.' You see, Puskas was the youngest amongst them and they called him 'Ocsi'.

Later on, another nickname was added: 'the Swabian', a reference to Puskas's German ancestry and – according to some – a tendency to be extremely careful with money.

Puskas: Some of the older brothers of the kids I played with had been picked up by the local club and drafted into its junior teams, around the age of twelve. So football talk was all around us. We picked up skill-training techniques from these older lads, learning one-touch or two-touch games and ball control. From about the age of six or seven we began to get a real feel for the ball, keeping it up endlessly with head or foot. But even before then, I think we'd already been gripped by a passion for the game that would remain with us all our lives.

It wasn't long before we were attracting a little fan club of our own in the neighbourhood. There were some really generous people around who seemed to like and encourage us at every turn; people like 'uncle' Jozseph. He was the local butcher who once offered a fantastic prize for the winners of a street match: a big savoury sausage. That gave the game between hungry, growing kids some real edge. Many years later, after the Uprising in 1956, that same butcher came to see me in Spain when I was playing for Real Madrid. He ended up staying for five years and working in my sausage factory there, but that's another story.

Joining Kispest as a 'junior'

Puskas: As time went by, we graduated naturally towards the local football club. At first we just helped around the place, cleaning boots, raking the pitch, whatever. In the afternoon we would get a ball to play with, and another perk was getting in free for proper league matches. One day in 1936, a fire destroyed part of the stadium and we did everything we could to help in the rebuilding. That was real communal effort, unlike the staged moments for the press during the building of the great Nepstadion *[the 'People's Stadium']* in 1953 when, as players of the national team, we were required to put in a couple of well-publicized days' work to show we were good communists.

Every year, someone from the Kispest Club would make it his business to run his eye over the youngsters. I remember a trainer, Nandor Szucs, having a look at us and choosing a few. My friend Jozsef Bozsik was picked but I insisted on joining him. Bozsik was eleven when the coach asked him to join Kispest as a junior, and told him to get a photograph taken so he could be registered with the club. I piped up: 'What about me? Jozsef and I always play together on the pitch and we get a lot of goals between us.' So Nandor Szucs told me to get a photo too, but I had to lie about my date of birth, giving 1925 instead of 1927. Officially you had to be over twelve to play in junior football, so I aged two years for a while and even had a different name. *[He was called 'Kovacs' which, like its English equivalent*

'Smith', is one of the most common surnames in Hungary.] A lot of people knew about this little fraud, even opponents, but no one seemed to mind.

My father

Puskas: By then my father was a semi-professional player, first for Vasas then at Kispest. He played as an attacking centre-half. He could earn some money with football but he also had to work part-time, so it was mornings at work, afternoons training. At various times he worked as a mechanic for the local railway company; then as a weighman in the Kispest slaughterhouse (where Bozsik's father also worked), and later he became the head book-keeper. Though our flat was small and fairly basic, I never heard my parents complaining; and anyway, we could see folks much worse off than ourselves.

In 1936, my father hung up his playing boots and became a coach, though he continued to work in the mornings. At Kispest, he soon took responsibility for four teams: the young juniors, the older juniors, the reserves and the first team. In reality he was the club manager.

Not only could we juniors get in to see the league matches, we could also watch the advanced training of the fully developed players. Just like kids do, we would immediately try to copy what they did. The truth is that that was the way we learned to play the game, both before and after we joined the club. But now we had a coach to lead us and I got my first decent pair of boots. The local shoemaker made them for me just before my first match with the juniors. They were a little big for me – to make them last longer – and I had to stuff the toes at first to make them fit. My feet got so sore after a match that I couldn't kick a ball for days afterwards.

The Kispest first team at that time was in the first division, amongst the very best, but usually occupying a mid-table position or lower. It wasn't a rich club like Ferencvaros, but we did have one or two internationals in the team. My favourites were Jozsef Nemes, a right-half, and Karoly Deri. I liked their style and flair. Nemes was a very intelligent player with perfect ball control; Deri was a great dribbler. We stole every footballing thing we could from these guys. I think it was crucial in our development, simply having the opportunity to watch good players at close quarters, training and playing the game. Hungary had reached the Final of the 1938 World Cup and that inspired a lot of players as well as us youngsters. I'm sure that's one of the reasons why Hungary produced so many good players who came through in the post-war years. We did know of some foreign footballers, like the Spanish goalkeeper Zamora, but when we played as kids together I always assumed the identity of a local hero, usually Nemes or Deri.

Until about the age of twelve I was quite small, but then I started to grow. I was always strong and very quick, running everywhere I went. But as we grew up, the games we played became more serious and the opponents stronger. Then, it wasn't enough to be able to control the ball and do a few tricks with it. So we started to do exercises that would build up our physical strength. I wasn't very tall, so I needed to be strong and quick and, starting early, I was playing with lads a bit older, which made me feel even smaller in comparison. So I adjusted my game to my circumstances. I looked for space and stayed well out of the way from the physical confrontations, where I wouldn't have been much use anyway. I learnt that lesson quickly and it has stood me in good stead ever since.

After training in the afternoon, we all got a glass of milk and some bread and butter to help build us up. Sometimes we misbehaved a bit, throwing stones at passing Ferencvaros supporters. As those of us who became juniors at Kispest got older – in our early teens – we started to read the game and began to attempt to realize ideas on the pitch. That junior team – all local lads – was a good side, one of the best in the country. We would knock in 130 to 140 goals a season. Almost every one of us made it to become first division players, an exceptional success rate, and of course a few of us went on to play for our country.

We were also very good mates and would do almost anything to help one another, both on and off the pitch. But we were ferociously competitive as well, screaming at each other during games, though there were no recriminations after matches. There were occasional fights during training, I remember the odd bleeding nose. But if my father arrived to ask what was happening, we said, 'Oh nothing, nothing at all.'

My father wasn't what you would describe as a strict coach. Generally, he was pretty cheerful though he was never satisfied, however well we performed. But he didn't have us all running around the pitch, engaged in boring training. It was the *ball* we loved, and we would do anything that involved playing with one. In a sense, we were unknowingly developing a very modern training routine: lots of one- or two-touch five-a-sides; shooting practice; rehearsals of set-pieces and so on. A few years later, after the war, we got into playing foot-tennis with benches in the middle of the court as a net. We had teams of two-to-four players each side and, as the loser had to buy dinner and wine for the winners, they could be real needle matches. I also found playing handball regularly in winter a very good training for football – you've got to be very sharp with quick reactions. That's how I met my wife, playing handball *[Puskas married Erzebet in 1951].* I liked her game and she liked mine.

My father was sensitive with me personally, never forcing things on me but letting my game develop quite naturally. The only thing he did go on about was my learning to kick the ball well with my right foot. I would say, 'If you kick with both feet, you fall on your arse!' But otherwise, he didn't interfere. Actually, I did learn to use my right foot but in match situations I only ever used that foot to kick a moving ball. If I could stop a ball, I used my left. Unfortunately, my father did not live to see the Golden Squad's greatest triumphs. Sadly he died in 1952, only forty-nine years old.

Szepesi: Puskas loved his father very much and was devastated by his early death. But I don't think Puskas ever really respected another coach, not in Hungary in his early days. He could be very awkward with some of those who took over at Kispest, and I think the roots of that lay in this very easy-going relationship he had with his first coach – his father. He did listen to him, I'm sure, but on the pitch he did as he liked and I suspect his father indulged him more than another coach might have done.

Friendship with Jozsef Bozsik

Puskas: Jozsef Bozsik and I were best friends. I was only three when his family moved into the flat next door to us; his was number 20, ours number 19. He was a year and a half older than me *[born November 1925]*, but because we were such close neighbours, we became good friends and developed a signalling system of 'wall knocks' to indicate: 'How about a game?'

Perhaps inevitably, but I'm sure not inaccurately, I remember those days with great warmth. They were very good times. My friendship with 'Cucu' Bozsik was so close that we were like brothers. We stayed together as kids, then as senior players for Kispest and Hungary for many years to come, right up to the 1956 Uprising when we were separated for the first time. There were five boys in the Bozsik family, all in one bedroom. They all played for Kispest, at various levels. Istvan played in goal and the other three were in the under-18s team, I remember. Of course, much later Cucu became coach at Kispest. *[Bozsik was manager of Kispest between February 1966 and August 1967.]*

He was a very quiet guy, Cucu. A slow-moving, relaxed person; very thoughtful, never in a rush. He loved football very deeply but, I think, in a way different to most of us. He never seemed to get excited, just didn't show it at all. Off the pitch, I don't think I ever saw him angry, but on it, if someone had clobbered him off the ball, he could break into a rage and threaten to leave the field. Sometimes I had to go after him and calm him down. He was a true friend to me in football and in life. In a match – maybe because we had played together from such an early age – we knew exactly where each other was likely to be, on or off the ball. We really could find one another without looking.

We were allowed to attend professional games at the Kispest ground, but getting into away matches was a different proposition. Bozsik and I pulled all kinds of tricks to get into grounds, from the tender age of five or six upwards. I remember we dug a tunnel once under the perimeter fence in a deserted corner of one ground, I can't recall which now. The soil was soft and sandy and we got sand right up to our ears that day. But our usual dodge was to don our junior kit, pick up some equipment in bags from Kispest's ground, and walk halfway across town to the opponents' ground where we walked in as large and official-looking as we could. We usually got in all right and, after the match, we had to trail back home with the bags. We hardly gave it a second thought. It was well worth it.

As young men we did everything together, even ran a shop at one time. That was around 1947 or 48, I think. Kispest wasn't a rich club and they couldn't pay us anything near the wage we were really worth. So Cucu and I were offered a local shop in the main road of Kispest. It was an ironmonger's, selling pots and pans. You should have seen us, we thought we had come into a fortune. But we'd only been running it for a few weeks when the government nationalized all small businesses. We got a little compensation but that was the end of our career as shopkeepers.

We spent all our free time together too, strolling around town, catching a film once or twice a week in the evenings. We always got the tram home and one time when we were paying our fare, we looked at one another and said: 'Why are we doing this? We could *run* home as easily and save some money too.' So that began a period when we would regularly race the tram home. It was a good distance, about two and a half kilometres, and at first we didn't have a hope of keeping up with the tram. But after a while, we started catching it up and then overtaking it. The local tram drivers enjoyed the whole thing enormously. We were sixteen years old and as fit as fleas.

My father was impressed with Bozsik too. He admired his calm maturity and came to love him like a son. If I was trying to convince my father that something happened at training, and I could see that he didn't believe me, I would say, 'Ask your friend Bozsik, he will tell you I'm right.' Of course, once my father became a coach, and eventually manager of the club, he was for a while directly in charge of us both.

First-team debut

When Puskas made his first-team debut at Kispest in 1943, his father was not then coaching the team. However, by the time Kispest/Honved won the league in 1949–50, Puskas was team captain and his father was team coach again.

Puskas: I was only twelve when war broke out and life got increasingly tough. Everyone was short of even the basic necessities and I remember swapping clothes for things like flour and meat. League football did continue for a while because Hungary initially didn't experience any fighting or bombing on home soil. But as the war reached its climax, things changed. The Hungarian government was an ally of the Nazis and more and more players were called up to fight on the Russian front. The 1943–44 season was the last we completed before the end of the war. That was the season I made my debut in the first team, only sixteen years old.

It was December 1943, and Kispest were preparing for a match with the league leaders and eventual champions Nagyvarad *[now a city in Transylvania, Romania called Oradea]*. Another Kispest player had been grabbed by the army and the club was running out of men. Bozsik had made his debut in the spring that year against the Budapest club Vasas, though the team lost and he was subsequently dropped. When he heard I was picked he was great, encouraging me and giving me confidence because I was pretty daunted at the prospect. Kispest were a severely weakened side and didn't have much of a chance against this team.

We played the match on Sunday 5 December and lost 3–0. I played again three days later, away to Diosgyor, and we lost 3–2. I finally got my first league goal at home to Kolozsvar *[now also in Romania, called Cluj]* on 12 December, in a match we drew 2–2.

According to the following Monday's edition of Nemzeti Sport, *Puskas was chided by some of the players in the dressing-room at half-time for holding the ball too much. They told him to pass it quicker. Kalman Vandor started his career as a sports journalist in Hungary at the end of the war. He remembers the young Puskas annoying some of the senior players at Kispest:*

Vandor: I was in the forces from 1943 to 1945, serving in an army hospital halfway between the Kispest and Ferencvaros grounds. There were quite a few Ferencvaros players in my unit and the hospital team often trained with them or at Kispest. That's when I first saw the youthful Puskas. He stood out even then amongst much older players, but there was some resentment amongst them about his constant talking and shouting during a match. No one disputed his talent, though. I thought him an excellent player but I had no idea that he would become a world-class player.

Puskas: I think I was the youngest player in the Hungarian first division and I was probably out of my depth. But I must say the Kispest players were never hard on me; they treated me as an equal and I learned to play for the benefit of the whole team. It wasn't long before Bozsik returned to the side, and I was never dropped from the first match onwards. It's funny but, even today, I'm very proud of that.

I was certainly lucky not to be old enough to get called-up. In a sense, football protected me from the war. I was so caught up with the game that I often forgot about it altogether. Looking back, I seem to have so much to thank football for in my life.

Life at the Kispest club

When I reflect on the financial arrangements in those days at Kispest, I can see how comparatively well-off I was, even though the pay was poor. Those were the days when we didn't even have a contract or fixed salaries. It sounds crazy now, but we would go and ask the chairman or financial secretary for money when we needed some. If the team did well, we got paid a little more. I think, in fact, they paid us individually, according to how well they thought we had played. But with Kispest being a fairly small club in those days, with gates of only around 2–3,000 spectators, there was never much to spare. Nevertheless, I always seemed to have enough and I think I earned more than my father at the time.

The club relied heavily on its 'sponsors', but these were not big businesses or anything like. They were, in fact, people like the local tailor who made the kits and tracksuits; the local shoemaker who made the boots we wore; the owner of a local restaurant where we had a meal after training on Tuesdays and Thursdays; the local butcher who provided meat, and so on.

I lived better than the average worker in Kispest. It is hard to remember the exact amount I was paid now, but I know I could afford the basics without difficulty. I certainly didn't complain about pay. I knew the club's sponsors weren't rich businessmen, only shopkeepers, and perhaps the owner of a small factory. But these people who helped the club were extremely enthusiastic about football and did everything they could to help Kispest.

The crowd at Kispest may not have been huge *[unlike at Ferencvaros or MTK]* but those who did come were very keen on their football. They had a real affection for the team and, even when we were losing, they kept cheering and encouraging us. They were a very knowledgeable crowd too, appreciative of the finer moves and passes in the game.

At the club and amongst the players, it did feel to me like being in a big family. It was a very different experience from the way things are in football today, I'm afraid. There seems to be very little real friendship in the modern game. Players today just come in, do their job and go home. In those days, after training we usually stayed together for the afternoon, having fun, drinking 'froccs' *[a cheap mixture of wine and soda water very popular with working-class Hungarians]* or having a beer and eating good spicy sausage. In 1945, new club rooms were opened in Kispest, just opposite the butcher's shop that regularly sent meat across for the players. Many a time, local performers and singers came along in the afternoon and we all sang our heads off and had a real laugh. It was great to be in such good company. The Kispest club was a genuine expression of the local community. I remember when we went to Vienna on our first football tour, our local sponsors – the shopkeepers – packed our bags with good food, especially sausages. Often, in the evenings, these men and other ordinary supporters would spend time with us, talking football, football and more football. I was very lucky to be amongst so many who were real lovers of the game.

The end of the war

On 19 March 1944, German troops occupied Hungary for the first time and prepared to face the advancing Russian armies from the east. That day, Puskas played in front of a 12,000 crowd when Kispest took on the biggest club in Budapest, Ferencvaros.

Puskas: Kispest played an away match against Ferencvaros. I was closely marked by a very experienced defender called Ferenc Rudas, who also played for the national team. I scored two. War planes were flying overhead throughout the match, but we played on regardless.

After this match, Puskas was heavily praised in the newspapers and described as a real talent. In the 1943–44 season, Kispest finished tenth in a league of sixteen; Puskas played eighteen matches and scored seven goals. The following autumn, many games were disrupted or abandoned because of bombing by Allied planes, aimed at the destruction of Hungarian industry. When the Germans eventually retreated west, they destroyed all the city's bridges across the Danube which joined Buda to Pest. In February 1945, Budapest was liberated by Russian troops.

Puskas: We came out of the cellars where we'd been hiding from the fighting for the city, and ran straight onto the football pitch. It wasn't long before some Russian soldiers turned up and wanted a game. They were quite skilful and we enjoyed the match. Next day they brought us flour but, though we were friendly with these soldiers, we still didn't dare to go out after dark. It was too dangerous.

There was no league football staged until the early summer after the Russians had liberated Budapest. It kicked off on 6 May but only involved the capital city's clubs, to avoid travelling. Kispest didn't play well and suffered some heavy home defeats, yet still managed to come fourth out of twelve.

Puskas: I remember we lost badly to Ferencvaros, 7–0, and I was sent off for a foul on that same Rudas. It was even worse against Ujpest, where we got whacked 8–0. Since those days I have never been in a team that conceded so many goals.

International debut

In the summer of 1945, on 19 and 20 August, the first post-war internationals were played against Austria and Puskas made his debut for the national team.

Puskas: There were two matches against Austria on consecutive days during August. Of course, Austria was the 'old enemy' on the football field as far as Hungarians were concerned. The two respective Football Associations had long-standing relationships and rivalries. It was a bit like the old England v Scotland matches. Anyway, the Austrians were invited to Budapest for the two games. Though times were hard in Hungary, they were much harder in Austria at the end of the war and they simply could not host an international match at the time. Everyone was very worked up about the prospect of two matches against our greatest rivals. It was a way of returning to normal after such terrible times.

The matches were played at the weekend, in front of packed, capacity crowds in Ferencvaros's stadium. It was an opportunity for the national team coaches to try a number of new players and different formations. It was the start of new life, and the atmosphere in the ground was incredibly intense. I made my international debut in the second match. We had won the first 2–0, and we won the second 5–2. I scored one of them. It was a team full of youngsters and after the match we had one of the best parties I can remember.

Gusztav Sebes, who would become the national coach of the Hungarian team in its greatest days, was then an assistant coach.

In his book, Happiness and Disappointment, *he writes of these matches against Austria:*

Sebes: 'Budapest was completely in ruins, not a single bridge standing over the Danube. Many of the players weren't in the best of condition, of course, but they still very much wanted to play. As coaches, we didn't have a great deal of choice when it came to selecting sides, but everybody was willing to play, if only for the guarantee of a week's full board and lodgings at a time when only coupons would buy you food.' (Sebes, 1981)

Puskas: There was only one more international match that year, in September at home against Romania. We won 7–2 and I got two goals. I was never out of the national team after that, not until 1956 when I left Hungary.

2

The Emergence of the Golden Squad

'By the time all these good players had settled down at Honved, we were becoming perhaps the finest club side in the world.'

After the war, the first general election in Hungary produced a coalition government dominated by conservatives (Smallholders' Party), but with the communists, social democrats and others playing a part. In 1946, Hungary proclaimed itself a republic and the first measures to abolish large estates and nationalize industry were implemented. A new government was formed two years later with Communist Party members occupying all the key posts, and a second election in 1949 – the so-called 'single slate' election which offered no choice but the communists – signalled the start of a regime dominated by Stalinists and controlled by the Soviet Union. The state security police, the AVH, was established. Almost immediately, 'show trials' began as native Hungarian communists – like Laszlo Rajk and his colleagues – were arrested and liquidated.

In 1946, the national football league restarted in Hungary.

Puskas became the regular captain of a Kispest team coached by his father. That season, Kispest finished fourth. Puskas travelled abroad for the first time with the national team in April 1946, to Vienna where Hungary lost 3–2 and he was substituted. He returned for the next game against Austria in Budapest on 6 October, a victory for the home side, 2–0. Puskas hit his first international hat-trick in the last match of that year, a 7–2 win over Luxembourg (a match not included in some international records).

During this period, some of the Hungarian football coaches who had achieved reputations before the war began to return home. Men like Marton Bukovi, who had spent years in Yugoslavia, and Bela Guttmann were attached to clubs like MTK, Ujpest and Kispest. At first the national team was managed by Tibor Gallowich, but soon Gusztav Sebes was appointed to chair a three-man 'coaches' committee' with Gabor Kleber, the former international player, and Bela Mandik, an experienced youth coach. The committee sent its representatives around the country looking for talent to recruit to the national team. In the process, they found players like goalkeeper Grosics and full-back Buzanszky, both from a small mining town in northern Hungary called Dorog.

Offers from abroad

Kispest continued to improve, and came second in the league in 1946–7. In May 1947 Hungary played Austria yet again, winning 5–2 in front of 38,000 fans at Ferencvaros's ground, with Puskas scoring. A week later, Hungary travelled to Turin where they were beaten by the reigning world champions, Italy. Puskas remembers that occasion for a number of reasons.

Puskas: We lost 3–2 to Italy and they got the winner in the last minute. I scored from a penalty in front of 70,000 fanatical Italian fans. The Italians were impressive with an attack led by Valentino Mazzola, who died so tragically with the Torino team in a plane crash a few years later, in 1949. Strangely enough, his son played against me in my last European Cup Final, in Vienna, nearly twenty years later. *[Sandro Mazzola scored twice in Internazionale's 3–1 victory over Real Madrid in 1964.]*

I remember this journey abroad particularly because, after the match, I was offered 100,000 US dollars – a huge sum – to join Juventus. Quite openly, two Italian guys walked over to me waving a piece of paper – a contract with $100,000 written on it. I was confused, flustered, and played for time. I asked them to write to me in Budapest with all the details and sure enough, within a few days, I got a letter outlining the whole proposal. It was a great deal of money for a young man like me, but in reality, I was not free to take the offer seriously.

It was not that I couldn't leave Hungary – at that time I probably could have – but it would have meant leaving behind my parents, sister and other relatives. This was no simple matter because my family was originally of German extraction, generations previously, and there were real fears about post-war retaliations in Hungary.

The Hungarian government's alliance with the Axis powers began in 1938. The Horthy administration had moved increasingly towards fascism, enacting anti-Jewish legislation. In deference to his new ally, Horthy granted special privileges for the ethnic Germans living in Hungary (some Hungarians changed their names back to their 'German' ones to take advantage) and, later on in the war, the Nazis were able to recruit some of them into the Volksbund and the SS. Other Hungarians, especially the communists, formed resistance movements and fought the fascists throughout the war. By 1947, in the post-war backlash, there was a wave of expulsions from Hungary of suspected 'German sympathizers'.

Puskas: With German ancestry, my family might have been forced to live somewhere they didn't want to or, worse, even sent to camps. My presence in Budapest made that prospect much less likely, so I gave up any plans I might otherwise have made. I didn't make a fuss about it; just took the decision and never regretted it. It was a clear choice: self or family. I loved them too much to leave them in danger.

International experience

The Hungarian national team continued to evolve and improve. During 1947 there were further victories over Bulgaria (9–0), Albania (3–0) and Romania (3–0). Sebes and his committee were still experimenting with different formations, but the nucleus of the great Hungarian squad was beginning to emerge, with Grosics, Bozsik, Hidegkuti and Puskas already involved.

Bozsik made his debut for Hungary while Puskas was away in South America. It took place on 17 August 1947, in the high-scoring defeat of Bulgaria. Bozsik had a tougher time getting into the national team than his friend. His game was misinterpreted by coaches and others. People said he was too slow, not physically but mentally. He would hold the ball for what seemed an unusual length of time, and he liked both to attack and defend. Eventually, observers realized that he only held onto the ball until the best position had developed. He then delivered it with stunning accuracy. Puskas's virtues, in contrast, were there for everyone to see immediately.

Szepesi: Puskas was gaining quite a reputation as he put on some remarkable performances. I remember one match against Ferencvaros in 1947 when he had to be taken off injured after a clash with his marker, Rudas. In fact Puskas was stretchered off, but reappeared on the pitch later with a huge bandage on his leg. Towards the end of the first half, he drifted into the penalty area and suddenly shouted 'Cucu now!' And Bozsik found him with a beautiful ball which he smashed into the net with his bandaged left leg. He limped through the second half, yet scored two more goals. Kispest won 3–0 and the crowd could hardly believe it.

[Puskas's wife-to-be, Erzebet, attended this match and was greatly impressed.]

In late May 1947, Kispest went on tour in France and Luxembourg. On the last day of the month, a special match had been arranged in Hungary between teams representing Budapest and Belgrade. The then national manager, Gallowich, had only agreed to Kispest's foreign tour providing Puskas was allowed to return early to play in the game, but Kispest sent him a telegram to say they did not want their player to travel back through Europe on his own. Gallowich threatened the whole club with a travel ban and Puskas was duly dispatched. He only just arrived back in time to go straight from the railway station to the warm-up on the pitch, telling stories about how he didn't have the cash to buy the last leg of his journey from Austria. Budapest beat Belgrade 3–2, and Puskas scored twice.

Around this time, more offers from abroad were emerging for other key Hungarian players. Exposure on foreign tours spread the word around Europe's footballing community and, at the end of Kispest's French tour, an offer of two million francs was made for Bozsik, who refused even to consider it. Ferenc Szusza, a talented striker in the post-war Hungarian squad was the object of an inquiry from Inter Milan, but his club Ujpest dismissed it. No one was quite sure what would be allowed under the new communist regime and what forbidden. Soon the authorities began to make their position plain, with announcements that no player of either first or second division status would be allowed to go abroad because it would weaken the national drive for sporting excellence. Scare stories appeared in the state-controlled press warning of 'agents' stalking Budapest (usually on behalf of Italian clubs) trying to arrange the smuggling-out of chosen players; or of disastrous journeys by young Hungarians trying to cross the Alps to footballing freedom in Italy, only to have their toes frozen off with frost-bite.

For Puskas, in the high summer of 1947, there was another foreign tour. It wasn't with the national team or with Kispest but with the Ferencvaros club, to South America. It was also an opportunity –

both for players and football authorities – to earn some much-needed foreign currency.

Puskas: I was invited on to the South American tour with Ferencvaros. A player called Szusza from Ujpest came too, along with another Kispest international, Meszaros, who joined Ferencvaros later that year. *[A small club like Kispest could only maintain two internationals on its books. The money from the sale of Meszaros would have been used to keep Puskas and Bozsik at the club].* It was a good side and we held the Mexican national team to a 3–3 draw. I got paid 1,500 dollars for this trip, which seemed a huge amount of money. Indeed it *was* a lot, because I bought a house in Budapest with it. I moved out when I got married but my sister has lived there ever since.

Ferencvaros were the league champions in 1947–48, with an attack featuring Budai, Kocsis and Czibor, names that would come to haunt Englishmen such as Walter Winterbottom, Billy Wright and Alf Ramsey. The MTK club, coached by Marton Bukovi, came second; their team included Palotas, Hidegkuti, Lantos and Sandor, all future members of the Golden Squad. Kispest came third. Puskas had scored 50 goals in 31 games, making him the league's top scorer for the first time.

Bela Guttmann

Bela Guttmann replaced Puskas's father as coach at Kispest in 1948. Guttmann was to become one of the most famous and influential of Hungarian coaches in the years to follow. He coached in Brazil after 1956 and achieved his greatest heights with Benfica when he won the European Cup in 1961, breaking the stranglehold that Real Madrid had exerted on the competition for the previous five years, and retained the trophy the following season having signed Eusebio.

At Kispest, Puskas and Guttmann had their problems: two such strong personalities were perhaps bound to clash.

Vandor: Guttmann refused to tolerate the sort of thing that Puskas's father had let his son get away with. Guttmann was a very serious guy, a good man at heart and a real expert in his field. The problem was – and it was well known – young Puskas was virtually running the Kispest team from about this time. His voice was the strongest (and it grew more powerful later when little Kispest became the army's mighty Honved). But Guttmann probably made mistakes too. He felt he had to be very strict, but with these tough kids at Kispest, a different approach was required.

At one away match against Gyor in the autumn of 1948, Guttmann was getting very worked up on the bench about the rough tactics adopted by one of his own Kispest defenders, Mihaly Patyi. From the sideline, he warned the player to calm down and finally lost patience and attempted to substitute him. But Puskas told the player to stay where he was. Patyi was more afraid of his team captain than of Guttmann, so he stayed on the pitch. Guttmann resigned immediately after the match and refused even to return on the train with the players to Budapest. Puskas regretted the incident and attempted to apologize, but it was too late. The club made no comment and Puskas's father was appointed coach again.

Vandor: By then, in the late 1940s, Puskas was the undisputed leader of the team. He used his power to protect and provide for the other players. I remember one occasion when tickets were being distributed to the players in the Kispest restaurant before a match. Everyone got two except Puskas and Bozsik, who got four. When Puskas found out, he stood up and said they wouldn't play unless everyone got equal numbers. He was irrepressible.

Puskas punished

In 1948, Hungary played nine international matches losing only twice, away to Austria and Bulgaria. By now, Puskas was receiving some very special attention from defenders trying to mark him. In the match in Sofia, he was constantly fouled in and around the penalty area. Eventually, in the second half, he hit out at two of the Bulgarians and both went off for treatment. Puskas was very prickly with Hungarian FA officials after the match when threatened with punishment, and there were some amongst them who clearly thought he was getting too big for his boots. On 18 November 1948, the FA disciplinary committee announced a one-year international match ban.

The editor of Nemzeti Sport *('National Sport'), renamed* Nepsport *('People's Sport') under the communist regime, explained the decision on the front page: Puskas had not given of his best in Sofia; he was too worried about getting injured and, when urged on by the bench, had replied, 'I want to be able to play next week too, thanks.' He had been 'impolite' to officials after the match as well. The editorial complained that his attitude was inappropriate 'for a sportsman of the people's democracy proceeding towards socialism. We cannot be blackmailed by threats to leave the country. This punishment is a warning not only to Puskas, but to others too.'*

Later that day, Puskas went to the offices of Nepsport *and an account of his 'self-criticism' was published the following morning. Puskas was quoted:*

'I was very saddened to learn of the FA's ban and I don't think I deserve it. I did behave badly in Sofia, but I was extracting just revenge for the kicking I was getting. I know I was wrong and shouldn't have insulted the officials after the match. I flew into a rage at the treatment I was receiving from (centre-half) Trinkov. I just lost my rag. At Gyor too, where I've been in conflict with the coach (Guttmann), I was too edgy about everything. This ban has sobered me up considerably; perhaps if it had come earlier, nothing would have happened at Gyor. As for leaving Hungary, I have never indicated any such desire. I have been approached by some clubs, but I'm not going anywhere. I don't think I am essential for the national team's success and my only wish is to get back into the team.'

*In addition to the one-year international ban, it was announced on 16 December that Puskas would be banned from league matches until 4 April 1949. In the event he was quickly forgiven and returned to play at the start of the spring season on 19 February. The international ban was never enforced either; he played against Czechoslovakia on 10 April, without having missed a single international match.**

It wasn't only Puskas who was getting into trouble with the authorities. Around this time, Gyula Grosics, the goalkeeper, had a much more serious brush with the law.

Grosics: In 1949, I attempted to leave Hungary with a group of other people. I was arrested by the AVH and spent a night at their headquarters. They didn't harm me but spent the night making various threats and I was terrified of what might happen. From then on, I was always regarded as 'unreliable'. (K&S)

Sebes and the development of the Golden Squad

In 1951, the state extended its grip on virtually all aspects of social and cultural life. The Stalinist government arrested more prominent 'native' communists, including Janos Kadar (who would later become the Party boss after the Uprising of 1956 and remain in power until his death in July 1989). Forced collectivization on the land took place; mass deportations and persecution of the Churches increased. A new law was passed which placed physical education

* Due to injury, Puskas did not play in two earlier international matches: against Bulgaria and Albania in August 1947.

and sports development as the sole responsibility of the state. A National Physical Education and Sports Committee was duly constituted and it became, in effect, a Sports Ministry through which the leading politicians controlled every significant sporting development. The football players – and all sportspeople – were exhorted to commit themselves fully to the sporting components of Hungary's first 'Five Year Plan' (1950–54), based entirely on the Soviet model. It included a vast construction programme, with the building of the Nepstadion at its core.

Grosics: Gusztav Sebes was deeply committed to socialist ideology and you could feel it in everything he said. He made a political issue of every important match or competition. He often said that the fierce struggle between capialism and socialism took place as much on the football field as anywhere else. In time, he was not only the national coach but also second-in-command at the Sports Ministry, with political connections that made him more powerful than his boss *[Gyula Hegyi]*. There was a telephone on Sebes's desk that connected him directly to Mihaly Farkas, head of the Hungarian armed forces and the AVH, and Farkas would call him with the latest instructions.

Gusztav Sebes had risen to power quickly. At the beginning of 1948, the national coach, Gallowich, who had managed the Hungarian team since the war, suddenly resigned, to be replaced by a three-man committee which included Sebes. This 'socialist' approach to football management soon foundered on personal rifts between the committee members, despite their long-standing mutual friendship, and all three resigned at the end of the year. In January 1949, Sebes was placed in sole charge of the national team, though he always insisted that he continued to take advice from his old colleagues.

Sebes's political star was rising too. In addition to his roles as national coach and Deputy Sports Minister, he also chaired the Hungarian Olympic Committee, an organization that earned enormous credit from the success of Hungarian athletes at the 1948

Olympic Games in London. Sebes was a communist of long standing, with an appropriate political pedigree: he had helped to organize car workers in the Renault factories of pre-war Paris, and in post-war Hungary he was a powerful figure in the trade union movement. In short, he was trusted by the regime's leadership.

Sebes liked to retreat to the mountains to think about the evolution of the national team. He read widely and acknowledged the influence of men like the Italian tactician Vittorio Pozzo and the Austrian coach Hugo Meisl. He remembered Jimmy Hogan too, the English 'master' of the pre-war MTK team, who had taught Hungary much of its early footballing knowledge. Sebes decided to develop not just a team but a squad of young players – a group that would contain the most skilful players of their generation, able to adopt a variety of tactical shapes. As their fame grew, this group became known as 'the Golden Squad'.

Under the communist regime, Sebes found considerable powers to co-opt people and players from league football to help his cause. The national team carried a high priority with the Party and its officials. Sebes invited all the first division coaches to a meeting where he unfolded his plan to recruit a squad consisting of the best young talent in the country. He wanted the coaches' full co-operation to identify and track these players; he even requested referees to keep him informed, and persuaded the Hungarian FA to establish a 'Friends of the National Players' club.

Under Sebes, the national team could play friendly matches on Wednesdays in the provinces to help develop the desired familiarity amongst his squad of players. Playing outside Budapest took the pressure off young players as the provincial crowds were more tolerant and patient than their big-city counterparts. Sebes could therefore use these regular fixtures to experiment with various tactical shapes and to identify the players who flourished best within them. He also made sure that the host clubs kept the gate receipts (and crowds of up to 15,000 were not unknown for these matches), which further fostered good relations.

Early tactical experiments

Sebes's first match in charge was not a happy occasion. It was the game against Czechoslovakia in Prague on 10 April 1949 when Puskas was returning from his 'ban'. After the defeat against Bulgaria in Sofia, Sebes wanted to tighten up the defence and use faster forwards. Up front, he wanted to play Czibor on the left wing and Budai on the right, with Kocsis at inside-right and Puskas inside-left (a forward-line that, with Hidegkuti at No. 9, eventually became the preferred choice). Others thought it too adventurous an attack and Sebes for the moment backed down, but he got his way with the defensive line-up: in front of the new young goalkeeper Turai were Rudas, Balogh, Bozsik, Borzsei and Zakarias. Hungary lost the match 5–2 and the new formation in defence – especially the thoroughly nervous performance from Turai – received heavy criticism, some of it from the same coaches who had changed Sebes's mind about his original plan.

The next game was against the 'old enemy' Austria on 8 May, and this time Sebes ignored everyone and picked his own team, including a forward-line of four teenagers plus Puskas:

Henni
Rudas   Balogh
Bozsik   Borzsei   Lakat
Budai   Kocsis   Deak   Puskas   Czibor

They won 6–1, with Puskas getting his second international hat-trick.

This display of attacking football, inspired by the wing-halves and the wingers, encouraged Sebes to experiment further. One of the things wrong with this team, Sebes believed, was that the players were drawn from so many different clubs. He wanted to follow in the footsteps of Pozzo and Meisl who both based their national teams around two particular clubs (Torino and Juventus for Italy, Rapid and Austria Vienna for Austria).

Sebes was already planning his side for the return match in Vienna. Neither of these two great rival nations had managed to beat the other 'away' for twelve years. But the next match was against Italy, whom Hungary had not defeated since 1925 (and to whom they had lost 4–2 in the 1938 World Cup Final in Paris). Sebes dropped Czibor, played Puskas on the left wing and brought in Szusza at inside-left, but the attack slowed down. The match was a 1–1 draw and Puskas later complained that he didn't like playing wide on the left. So Sebes dropped Puskas for the next match (v Sweden) and brought Czibor back in. Deak got injured during the game and Puskas came on but, despite leading 2–0 with ten minutes to go, the Hungarians only managed a draw. Sebes noted how the Swedish fans had kept up the pressure on their team right to the finish and the players had responded. Still unhappy with his formation, Sebes continued to experiment, bringing in Lantos to play against Poland in the summer (but dropping Budai and Kocsis to the 'B' team) and winning the match 8–2.

Sebes rescues Lorant

The return game with Austria in Vienna was scheduled for autumn 1949, but Sebes planned the match in detail for months beforehand. In particular, he was looking for a strong, skilful centre-back and the young Vasas player Gyula Lorant had caught his eye. There was only one problem: Lorant had got himself into trouble with the political authorities and was in detention in a labour camp.

Lorant's story illustrates some of the problems faced both by footballers in Eastern Europe and by the regimes trying to retain their most talented players. Most football clubs in post-war Hungary – as elsewhere in the communist bloc – were not rich institutions. They could hardly afford to pay their players anything other than small expenses and consequently most players also had full-time jobs, often losing pay when absent through travelling with their clubs.

Hungarians returning from the West would tell players how much their services were worth in places like Italy and Spain, and naturally some were tempted to try to leave Hungary to pursue careers abroad. On this particular occasion, Lorant and around fourteen other players from different clubs secretly planned to leave Hungary and form a team under the name 'Hungaria', presumably with the intention of touring around Europe playing lucrative friendlies. Three of the 'ring-leaders' of this 'conspiracy' – Lorant among them – were arrested and placed in detention camps.

Sebes went straight to the Interior Ministry where Janos Kadar was then in charge. Sebes told Kadar that he needed Lorant for the Vienna game and that giving players like Lorant the chance to represent their country would help change attitudes amongst others. Kadar asked him whether he was not concerned that, once in Austria, Lorant would abscond anyway. Sebes replied that there were some in Budapest who might hope that happened, if only to discredit the national coach himself.

In the event, Lorant played in Vienna – an illustration of Sebes's political clout. Outside the dressing-room before the match, the tall centre-half whispered his thanks to Sebes for enabling his release from the camp. He played brilliantly and began a long and successful career at the heart of the Hungarian defence. The match was won 4–3 with Puskas scoring the winner, a penalty with only minutes remaining. Back home, the Hungarians were ecstatic with this first away victory over their great rivals for twelve years.

Because of a technicality, Czibor was unable to play against the Austrians. During the tactical discussions on the morning of the match, Sebes emphasized the importance of cutting off the supply to the great Austrian midfielder Ocwirk. He told the assembled squad that he had thought of deputing Puskas to mark Ocwirk, but he knew how Puskas hated to be tied down to a particular role and gave the job to Deak. This apparently fired Puskas up so much that he not only marked Ocwirk out of the game but also led the attack with ferocious enthusiasm.

This great victory in Vienna strengthened Sebes's hand with the political authoritiees. The financial plight of players like Lorant brought home the necessity for the government to make some special provision for national players. Accordingly, in addition to their salaries as workers, they were allowed an extra sum of 600 forints, designated as 'calorie money' to assist their special diet. All this, of course, took place against a backdrop of severe economic hardship and post-war rationing, confirming the special priority that the Hungarian authorities accorded to football.

The national team's performances continued to improve during 1949 with Puskas scoring 11 goals in 8 internationals, with only one defeat. That year the players were given the honour of being the first citizens to pass over the rebuilt Chain Bridge in Budapest, one of many that were destroyed in 1945 and subsequently reconstructed.

Kispest becomes 'Honved'

At the end of 1949, the Hungarian Ministry of Defence proposed that, just as in the Soviet Union, the 'people's army' should have its own football club, a leader in its field, able to promote national pride and cohesion amongst the Hungarian soldiers. The obvious choice was Ferencvaros, the greatest and most popular club in the land. But there was one insurmountable political problem: Ferencvaros had a history of nationalist and fascist associations. During the war, the club had consistently supported right-wing elements and, at one stage, even had a fascist leader on the board. The club also had a long tradition of independence and many amongst its most fanatical supporters were unhappy with the new communist regime. Sebes felt that any attempt to take Ferencvaros over as the 'army' club would be doomed to failure. In the end, little Kispest – with crowds of a mere 4,000 – was chosen to become the mighty 'Honved', 'defenders of the motherland'.

Puskas: I remember well the decision to nationalize the private football clubs in 1948–49. It was certainly the case that the commercial sector couldn't keep them going, as it didn't really exist any more. There was some panic amongst the country's football clubs, both great and small, as they wondered what would be their fate. The typical solution in the socialist bloc was to have the clubs 'sponsored' by different political ministries, trade unions, factories, mines and state institutions. As a player, it didn't make a drop of difference to me; but for Ferencvaros, the way it was arranged meant a massive drop in status for the club. It lost its traditional colours, even its name for a while, and ended up with a decidedly unglamorous sponsorship by the state food-workers' union (EDOSZ). I think it was a disgrace what happened to this once-great club which, after all, was supported by virtually ninety per cent of Hungarian football fans. Immediately, other clubs with better political connections began to pick off Ferencvaros's best players. First to go were the goalkeeper Henni and a striker called Deak, both players in the national squad. It was Ujpest Dozsa – sponsored by the powerful Ministry of the Interior – who got them.

One advantage of choosing Kispest, of course, was the fact that two of the national team's most important players – Puskas and Bozsik – were already well established there. It was a comparatively minor, working-class club with a politically clean bill of health and a small, if devoted, home crowd. As Sebes was planning to house his national squad in two clubs only, it served his purpose that Kispest should be one of them. But the other club could certainly not be Ferencvaros.

At this point, Sebes began to worry that his plan to concentrate his best players in just two club sides might fall apart. He could see what was going to happen, with various powerful political sub-groups squabbling to divide the best players up between their sponsored teams. He sought to persuade the party bosses that central control was required, not a free-for-all amongst the backers of the leading clubs, and in the end he got his way.

Puskas: Lorant duly arrived at Kispest/Honved, and one day

Budai and Kocsis approached me and talked about the possibility that they might come to Honved. I told them they couldn't make a better move, and I was certainly excited at the prospect of playing with them. Of course, Kocsis was a big Ferencvaros fan from way back, and he remained so all his life. Everybody knew it, too. But he was a great sportsman and I'll never forget some of the goals he scored *against* Ferencvaros. It was tough for their supporters, though. As it developed, the system was also tough on some very good players in clubs other than Honved. They had no chance of forcing themselves into the national team, because we at Honved knew each other's game so well.

I used to advise the chairman at Honved about the players we should be getting to make the perfect team. Soon Grosics came along, and Czibor arrived the following year from Csepel. I suppose I was a little naive at the time, I certainly didn't realize just how much it was Sebes who was actually pulling the strings, drawing together his Golden Squad. The decision to change my club's name was announced on 18 December 1949, during the celebration of Kispest's 40th anniversary. For me, whether it was 'Kispest' or 'Honved' made no difference. Football is football, regardless of names.

Sebes had one invaluable tool for manoeuvring young men into the 'army' club: he could conscript them. It was especially easy in the case of players like Budai, Czibor and Kocsis, who were at the age of compulsory national service (and who would undoubtedly prefer to play football rather than play at soldiery). The other club chosen to hold most of the rest of Sebes's national squad was MTK (known at various times as 'Bastya', Voros Lobogo ('Red Banner') or 'Hungaria'). This Budapest club was backed for a period in the early 1950s by the powerful state secret police, the AVH – Hungary's equivalent of the Soviet KGB.

Czibor, Kocsis and Budai

Zoltan Czibor was from a family of railway workers in Komorom, a town on Hungary's border with Slovakia. By the age of eighteen, he was driving a train for a living and playing football, along with two older brothers, for the local team in the third division. He was spotted by a national youth team coach and played in a regional (Transdanubian) youth team before making his debut in the national youth team on 11 May 1948. He was a very quick left-winger. That was enough to attract the interest of some of the bigger clubs and shortly afterwards he chose to join Ferencvaros, playing thirty matches for the club during their championship-winning season, 1948–49. His debut for the national team, on 8 May 1949, was also an auspicious occasion with Hungary thrashing Austria 6–1.

Czibor: 'After our championship-winning season, there was an attempt to ban Ferencvaros from playing at all *[probably because the club was becoming a sanctuary for dissidents who used the anonymity of the club's huge crowds to express opposition to the regime]*. There was a strange atmosphere throughout the club and, in the end, we were banned from playing any home matches. I was glad to get away, and for the next two years I played for a club called Csepel. As soon as I reached the age for military service, in 1953, I was called up to play for Honved. There can be little doubt the advantages of getting so many good players together in one team as the nucleus of the national squad. The reason why nobody in the world could beat us for four years *[1950–54]* was partly because so many of us played for one club. We loved playing and we knew how important it was to the whole nation for us to provide some joy at a time when many other things were very hard. Off the pitch, we were all very different guys, but on it sometimes things almost approached perfection. We knew each other's game inside out.' (Bocsak, 1983)

Sandor Kocsis was a precocious footballing-talent. He spent his early teens in war-torn Budapest, sometimes practising with a rag ball in the cellars of houses during bombing raids. As soon as the war was over, his father took him down to Ferencvaros, which was very close to the Kocsis family home. He was the first post-war youngster to register for the junior team and, on 26 May 1946, made his debut for the Ferencvaros first team at the age of sixteen against a Kispest side that included Puskas.

Kocsis was a tall, gangly lad and he lacked weight. The club tried to help build him up with special food parcels delivered to his home, and his father was given a local bar to run. His debut in the national team, like Czibor's, was a very promising one: in front of 45,000 Hungarian fans he scored two in the 9–0 defeat of Romania in June 1948. Kocsis gained a reputation as a fine header of the ball – he became known as the 'golden head' of the Golden Squad in later years, although Hungarian fans called him 'cube-head'. As soon as he came of conscription age, in 1950, he was given the 'choice' of playing for Honved or serving as a soldier on a border-post. Though he joined Honved, his heart always belonged to Ferencvaros and everyone knew it. Sometimes when he arrived at a restaurant in Budapest, the band would stop whatever they were playing and launch into a Ferencvaros song.

Puskas: Kocsis didn't really want to join Honved, which was understandable. Me, Bozsik and others tried to persuade him that it was better than soldiering. He was a very thin boy, three years younger than me, and we didn't get on particularly well at first. He loved the game – a great header of the ball and hungry for goals – but he liked to have a good moan at times. We did become friends in the end. Budai's move to Honved was much easier in comparison.

Budai: 'When I got called up for the army, I was sad to leave Ferencvaros but the choice of playing for Honved or spending a few years on a distant border-post was no choice at all, really. Kocsis and I talked about it together and chatted to Bozsik who assured us that things were fine at the club. By far the worst thing was not being able to fully explain our situation to the fans. Poor old Kocsis's dad had been given a bar to run by the club and was in an even worse situation.' (Bocsak, 1983)

Kocsis became very friendly with Laszlo Budai, a quick and skilful right-winger and an important source of supply for Kocsis's aerial goals. The same youth coach who had spotted Czibor also found Budai, playing for a small club in Budapest, and both of them arrived at Ferencvaros at around the same time in 1948. These three young players – two wingers and a centre-forward – often stayed on after training at the club, constantly rehearsing set-pieces and crosses to Kocsis from either flank. Just like Puskas and Bozsik, they developed an understanding on the pitch matched by friendship off it, and when they became the first choice forward-line of the national team (along with Puskas and Hidegkuti), these close empathies flowered into some of the best football the world had witnessed.

Budai: 'I was twenty, Kocsis and Czibor were both nineteen. We weren't born perfect players but we worked very hard together, practising so much with each other that we really did know without looking where any one of us would be on the pitch. In those days we never seemed to tire of training together and we would often play until dark or until we had perfected a move we were working on. If it didn't work out during a real game, it was back to the practice pitch for more. I'm not exaggerating when I say we would rehearse something 100 or even 150 times until it was just right. Our friendship just grew alongside.

'My debut for the national team coincided with Czibor's when we beat Austria 6–1. If you ask me why the "Golden Team" was so good, the answer is that it was an enormously talented squad, with five or six world-class players and a world-class coach in Gusztav Sebes. There is luck, too. Perhaps Sebes was fortunate to lose that first match 5–2 against the Czechs, because it forced him to look for a young team he could develop. Mind you, there were good and bad sides to most of us being in Honved. We certainly got to know each other's play very well and were paid as army officers – 1,600 forints a month at the time – even though we only had to play football. But it could be a bit of a hot-house with so many egos around. I mean, some of these guys were the best players in the world and they wanted things their own way. Puskas and Kocsis became great rivals. They were crazy, so hungry for the ball. Sometimes I'd be tearing down the wing and look up to see Puskas pointing with his thumb down for a ball to his left foot, while Kocsis was screaming for one to his head. I told them: "You guys need two balls to play with".'

Playing for Hungary, Ferenc Puskas and Sandor Kocsis formed the most potent international striking partnership of all time. By October 1956, they had scored 160 goals for Hungary between them – more than many entire national teams over the same period – with Puskas getting in his 84 appearances for Hungary and Kocsis, with 75 in 68 matches, scoring at an even higher average rate than his partner. (Puskas's statistics are the subject of dispute, with some sources indicating 85 goals in 84 international matches, or 85 goals in 88 internationals including two for Spain in four matches. Whichever figure applies, he remains the all-time top scorer at international level.)

Kocsis's family were never very happy with their son's treatment, at least in comparison with Puskas. They felt the team captain soaked up all the limelight, and they would say disparagingly of Puskas that he only had one foot when Sandor had two and his head as well. There is even a story that Kocsis's mother went to the Sports Ministry to complain that Puskas was making more money than her son. The truth was that Puskas had a much sounder grasp of his own 'public relations' than the rather introverted Kocsis. Puskas was also a better, or rather bolder, smuggler.

A little smuggling

Until 1950, most of the Hungarian international players were still professionals, getting paid a fairly low wage by their clubs. Indeed, Hungary's national football team was banned from the 1948 Olympics because their players were considered to be professionals.

Szepesi: The system changed after 1950 and all the players were given jobs. Some were placed in the army, like Puskas and Bozsik for example. Hidegkuti's job was in the Ministry of Light Industry; others worked for various state enterprises. But they were all sham jobs, so to speak. Some of them did go into work for, say, four hours a day. Hidegkuti and Zakarias did that, I believe, but the majority only went to work to pick up their wages. I know one who always sent someone in to collect his wage packet. He would say, 'Why should I go in there? I've never been there in my life and I don't know a soul there.'

Budai: 'We lived well in comparison to the average worker. We could even afford some "luxuries", but not from the salaries or bonuses we were getting. It was the smuggling that added that bit extra. It was generally condoned by the authorities. When we travelled abroad as the national team (at a time when it was very difficult for most Hungarians to leave the country at all), we would get "commissioned" to bring certain things back, things which were virtually unobtainable at home. Occasionally we would go too far and Puskas would get called in by the Defence Minister, Mihaly Farkas, one of the three most powerful members of the Communist Party politburo, and told to cool things down. Once, Puskas suggested to Farkas that we be paid decent salaries instead of these ill-defined "perks", but he was told it wouldn't go down too well with the miners and factory workers if we were paid anything like what we were worth on the open market. So the part-time smuggling continued.'

Vandor: They couldn't be properly rewarded or given hard currency, so the smuggling became an accepted thing. They could make some money from it. I remember once asking Puskas to bring me back some Wilkinson razor blades, which he did. But I had to pay for them, it wasn't a free service. They just said 'nothing to declare' at the borders and came straight through, and even if by chance a suitcase full of tights was discovered, Puskas could usually sort things out. Most of the team members took advantage of this, even to the point of helping supply machine parts and components to factories unable to obtain these things any other way.

Budai: 'I remember Hidegkuti was once asked to bring a suitcase full of sewing-machine needles back with him. He was struggling to get it on to the train and Sebes stopped to give him a hand. The coach found he could hardly lift the case and he wanted to know what the hell was in there. Hidegkuti explained what it was and that it was not a 'personal' business but vital supply parts for a factory. Sebes certainly checked it all out when we got back to Budapest.'

Szepesi: For a time, the Chief of Customs was actually a member of the board at Honved, which I'm sure helped smooth things out. The players got up to some fantastic tricks at a time when everybody else suffered enormous restrictions. I remember one occasion when the Customs Chief was travelling on the train with the team returning from a match in the West. The lads had literally hundreds of watches stuffed in various suitcases, especially Sandor and Puskas who'd set up a great smuggling partnership. As they approached the Hungarian border from Vienna, Puskas distracted the Customs Chief in the corridor while the others transferred all the watches to the Chief's baggage. Of course, his stuff wasn't even glanced at by his own officers, but after they'd gone, Puskas and the rest opened his bag to show him what he'd 'smuggled'. The old boy nearly had a heart-attack.

Lajos Tichy didn't join Honved until 1954; he played centre-forward between Puskas and Kocsis. He was just eighteen years old at the time and had been playing previously for second division Locomotive Budapest (the Railway Club).

Tichy: I had already heard rumours about their smuggling, and all my friends were impressed with my prospects when I was moved to Honved. (They were also very curious to know about the relationship between Puskas and Kocsis, who were often seen shouting at each other on the pitch.) Puskas was always very polite with the customs officers at the border. He would approach them ahead of us to soften them up, sometimes with a signed ball for one of the senior officers. I soon thought I was the bravest smuggler of all, bringing in sixty pairs of nylons a time, until I discovered the others were bringing in three thousand.

In the army

Puskas: By the time all these good players had settled down at Honved, we were becoming perhaps the finest club side in the world. We won the league title even before that, in the 1949–50 season, and we won a 'half league' as well when, in order to synchronize our season with the Russians, *[i.e. spring to autumn]*, we changed the schedules. The other 'national' club, MTK, won the title next time around. They had a coach called Marton Bukovi who had constructed a brilliant team which provided mainly the reserve pool of national team players, although some, like Hidegkuti, were first-team choices. They kept us on our toes, as for each position there was a perfect substitute who was used to playing in exactly the same tactical formation and so on. Honved and MTK were head and shoulders above the remainder of the league and each year, in reality, it was only a battle between the two of us: the army versus the secret police.

'My father was a semi-professional player, first for Vasas, then at Kispest.' The infant Puskas with his father, third player to his right. *(Hungarian Museum of Sport)*

'My father was quite sensitive with me personally . . . letting my game develop naturally.' The Kispest Juniors Team, with Puskas standing furthest left in the back row of youngsters and his father in the striped suit. *(Hungarian Museum of Sport)*

'I did learn to use my right foot but only ever to kick a moving ball.'
(Hungarian Museum of Sport)

'At the club and among the players, it felt like being in a big family.' Puskas is kneeling second from right. *(Hungarian Museum of Sport)*

'I liked her game and she liked mine.' Puskas married Erzebet in 1951. *(Hungarian Museum of Sport)*

'Along with a lot of other sportsmen, we were placed into the army's "Sports Company".' Bozsik at the microphone in 1950. *(Hungarian Museum of Sport)*

Football propaganda: Puskas, second from left, and Bozsik, far right, present a medal to a worker who, like them, produced more than the norm. *(Hungarian Museum of Sport)*

Puskas training at Craven Cottage two days before the Wembley match. *(Hulton Getty)*

Two teams walk out at Wembley, 1953. Billy Wright: 'We should be allright here, Stan, they haven't got the proper kit.' *(Popperfoto)*

The 7-1 scoreboard. Johnny Haynes: 'I was only on the bench, thank god.' *(Hungarian Museum of Sport)*

Gil Merrick: 'Never before in the whole of my career had I picked the ball out of the net seven times.' Puskas beats Merrick.' *(Popperfoto)*

'Leibrich caught me from behind, my leg went and I had to be taken off.' The injured Puskas on the pitch, World Cup, 1954. *(Hungarian Museum of Sport)*

Santos of Brazil, left, and Bozsik, both sent off during the 'Battle of Berne'. *(Hungarian Museum of Sport)*

Soldiers prevent the Hungarians from entering the stadium, 1954. Sebes: 'I got hit with the butt of a policeman's rifle as I tried to explain that we were the Hungarian team to play in the final.' *(Hungarian Museum of Sport)*

Grosics: 'If someone was to wake me up tomorrow morning and remind me of that match, I'd burst into tears.' Puskas congratulates Germany's Fritz Walter, 1954 World Cup. *(Popperfoto)*

There were some remarkable matches between Honved and MTK. They liked to score goals against each other just for fun. On one famous occasion still talked about in Budapest today, at the end of the 1954 season with Honved already crowned champions, the two teams produced a fantastic game: 7–3 to Honved at half-time and 9–7 at the final whistle.

Puskas: At Honved, we were the best. In the 1952 season we never lost a league match, dropping just a few points from the odd draw. Along with a lot of other sportsmen, we were placed into the army's 'sports company'. There was, at first, an attempt to impose some kind of army discipline upon us and we did spend the first three months living in a barracks and parading around in uniform. We even had to get up at six in the morning, but we soon persuaded the authorities that it wasn't healthy for sportsmen to be up at such an hour. We had to learn the basics of marching, saluting and so on, but after three months we were allowed to commute from home. Bozsik and I got promoted to the rank of lieutenant – God knows why – and after about a year and a half, all pretence was abandoned and we were dismissed from the barracks. I became the chief spokesman for the football players, at least those from Honved. If there were any problems, I would discuss them with the senior officers.

Tichy: When I joined the army and played for Honved in 1954, I was allowed to leave the barracks to train at any time. But on the first day there I had to get up at five in the morning, so later on that day I complained to Puskas. He said, 'Don't sleep here,' and arranged everything. In reality, I was only in the army for one day. I was a soldier only on paper.

Szepesi: Puskas always put on his army uniform if he wanted to arrange anything for his team-mates. Money problems, accommodation, hiccups at the customs, he could sort out just about anything in those days. He would arrive at the Defence

Ministry and get called in ahead of much more senior-ranking officers. He never seemed to get fazed. But apart from these occasions, he hardly ever wore the uniform at all.

Tichy: I remember Czibor got into serious trouble after a bad scene in a restaurant. He had a vitriolic, public argument with a waiter and some army officers wanted to see Czibor banned as a punishment. But Puskas made one of his visits to the Defence Ministry and nothing came of it.

Puskas: It was virtually impossible to keep us under military discipline. The officers were football crazy and conveniently overlooked any indiscretions. We even signed our own leave permits and wandered around town, drinking wine in bars. It was sheer embarrassment for the officers when we got caught. We were national heroes to many people – army generals amongst them – and they didn't want to take any action over these little adventures.

There were other sportsmen 'in the army' like us. We got on particularly well with the boxers and wrestlers, who often invited us to 'friendly' matches on five-a-side pitches. They were bruising battles sometimes, as these guys kicked lumps out of us. But the really great thing about being in the army's 'sports company' was the camaraderie and sometimes deep friendships which developed between us footballers and the other sportsmen. We had a ball together, we really did.

3

The Tactical Revolution

'The hardest thing was to find a good, central striker . . . somebody who was technically sophisticated, tactically aware, skilful and prolific.'

The tactical developments in Hungarian football during the early 1950s – when witnessed on home soil by the British public – did indeed seem revolutionary. But, naturally enough, the prototype 4–2–4 which emerged under the leadership of Sebes and his players was an evolution from a tactical dialogue that had been developing in Europe (particularly central Europe) since the late 1920s. The Hungarian innovations concerned primarily the role of the 'deep-lying centre-forward' – an advanced midfield play-maker operating within a very fluid system – which had its origins in much earlier footballing times.

Early football tactics

Decades before the Hungarians started playing the game, football tactics had been evolving in Britain. Association football emerged in the mid-nineteenth century from the English public schools and, initially, tactics and team formation were largely shaped by the relationships between the schoolboys who played the game. At most public schools, the prefects – older boys, mostly from aristocratic backgrounds – were highly autonomous and responsible for much of the school discipline. The prefects were served by selected younger boys – fags – and the football field was a stage upon which the power relations between fags and prefects were regularly enacted.

Football was often compulsory and organized entirely by the prefects; but only they were allowed to take an active part in the game as 'attackers'. This meant that up to two hundred fags were required to defend the line, or 'keep goal', while all the attacking was carried out by the prefects who spent the entire game crashing into the opposing line of fags. Consequently, it is hardly surprising to find that in the earliest stages of the development of association football, following the establishment of the Football Association in 1863, the first 'team formations' featured but one defender, a goalkeeper and nine attackers.

The formation looked like this:

goalkeeper
★

defender
★

attackers
★ ★ ★ ★ ★ ★ ★ ★ ★

Fig. 1

The aristocratic ex-public schoolboys who dominated the earliest stages of the game's development did not play with a view to 'defending' (who wanted to be a fag?) or even to co-operating much with the other players on their own side. Dribbling was the primary skill, along with speed, balance and the strength required to withstand the buffeting from the opposition while retaining possession. Team-mates had to remain behind the player in possession to avoid being 'offside', though from the 1860s onwards, FA rules defined 'offside' as applying only if the player was nearer his opponents' goal-line than the ball (at the moment the ball is played) unless there were three *opposing players nearer their own goal-line than he is.*

The invention of 'passing'

In the game's early days, passing the ball was an extreme rarity before the Scots footballers shattered the original, aristocratic version of the game in which individualism featured so prominently. They discovered that the ball could be moved towards the opponent's goal much more quickly and effectively by passing it from defence, through midfield, to attack. The English learnt the hard way, winning only two, and losing ten, of the first sixteen matches between these oldest international rivals in the football world.

*An abundance of attackers did not necessarily mean plenty of goals. When the world's first international match took place in Glasgow in 1872, England took the field with eight forwards, one half-back and one full-back (plus the goalkeeper); Scotland fielded a mere six attackers (***Fig. 2***). Yet, with fourteen forwards between them, neither team managed to score a goal that day.*

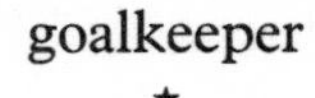

right-wing inside-right two centre-forwards inside-left left-wing

★ ★ ★ ★ ★ ★

Fig. 2

The second centre-forward

The crucial position for the subsequent development of tactics was that of the second centre-forward. It was the re-positioning of this player that moved the game forwards (or backwards, depending on your point of view) throughout the following century of football. The Scots quickly realized that the twin central strikers overlapped to their mutual disadvantage. They tried to dovetail the two, playing one just behind the other (in 'the hole', as it is often described today), but increasingly the deeper player found himself dropping back further, until he lost his 'forward' title altogether and became a true 'centre-half' (**Fig. 3**).

In the late 1870s, the Cambridge University team began to experiment with three half-backs, and by the time Preston North End were winning the world's first League and Cup double in 1889 (with their imported 'Scottish professors'), most teams were assuming the 5–3–2 shape. It came to dominate the tactics of the game all over the world for the next forty years. It was called the 'pyramid' formation, for obvious reasons.

Fig. 3

The withdrawal of the second centre-forward into midfield was 'a cellular cleavage' – as the Austrian journalist Willy Meisl described it – of the old central attacking role. In midfield, this new No. 5 position required considerable stamina, good ball-control and a striker's instincts too. The player was expected to 'make play' by feeding the forwards; then support the attack as well; to score goals arriving late in the penalty area; yet tackle opponents when his defence was under pressure. It was the kind of role that Bryan Robson would play for Manchester United and England during the 1980s.

The pyramid formation spread, along with the rules of the game, to wherever association football lodged. It seemed the only way the game should be played. It allowed for a strong emphasis on attack but, given the three-man offside law which prevailed at the time, forwards had to concentrate carefully and time their runs accurately to penetrate good defences.

In Hungary

It is said that a Hungarian student returning from England imported football into Hungary. Before the turn of the century, matches were being staged in Budapest involving teams from the city's oldest club: Budapesti Torna Club (BTC).* Football had already penetrated

* One of those who played in 1897, Alfred Hajos, lived long enough to advise on the construction of the great Nep Stadium over fifty years later, the ground where the Golden Squad performed some of their greatest feats, including the 7–1 thrashing of England in 1954.

Austria before the turn of the century and, perhaps inevitably, given the close relations between both countries within the Austro-Hungarian Empire of the Hapsburgs, Hungary's first international match was against a Viennese XI. It was the start of the fierce rivalry of Mittel-Europa.

The first English club to come to Hungary, Richmond FC in 1901, hammered BTC 6–0 and a 'national' team was beaten 4–0. Southampton were the first professional team to visit Budapest, in the same year, and they put seven past Hungary without reply. But the Hungarians learned fast. A full England team only won 4–2 eight years later, and in 1934 the inventors of the game lost to the Hungarians for the first time, 3–2 in Budapest.

In Hungary the pyramid formation was the only tactical shape adopted at first. British coaches had begun to arrive there as early as 1911, when a Scotsman called Robinson started work with the MTK club in Budapest. But by far the most influential British coach was the legendary Jimmy Hogan. He arrived via a sojourn in Austria where Hugo Meisl introduced him to the burgeoning Viennese football scene, and it was there that Hogan realized how primitive were the training methods he had seen in England. With Meisl, he worked out the first modern training-routine for professional players. The outbreak of war in 1914 threatened Hogan with internment in Austria, so he was smuggled to Budapest for the duration, where he began a long and fruitful partnership with one club in particular: MTK. It was Jimmy Hogan who established a tradition of English coaches at MTK that lasted for many years, and it is he who links the traditional attacking English game to the tactical revolution that occurred in Hungary thirty years later. Though he went back to Vienna after the war, Hogan returned again to MTK in 1925, just as the three-man offside law was about to be changed.

The new offside law

It happened on 13 June 1925 in Paris, and it was the British who insisted on the change. In England particularly, club directors were getting worried about declining gates at league matches, after an initial boom in attendances following the end of the First World War. The three-man offside law was held to be the culprit and there was some truth in the complaint that defences were operating the 'offside trap' more and more effectively. But there were no complaints from either supporters or club directors on the continent; neither were there any from the extremely widespread amateur game in England. Regardless, the members of the International Board of FIFA, eight out of ten of whom were British, forced the rule-change which now required – as it still does today – only two players (usually the goalkeeper plus one) between opponent and goal-line to play an attacker onside.

In England, the impact on the number of goals scored was immediate, as defences struggled to adjust to the new offside law: nearly 1,700 more goals were scored the following season (1926), an increase of almost forty per cent on the previous year. But ironically, the opening of the floodgates led directly to the kind of 'safety-first' football that would plague the English game throughout what is still regarded by many as its 'golden age'. One man more than any other, ominously often described as the 'godfather' of modern managers, was responsible for popularizing a new defensive approach: Herbert Chapman of Arsenal.

Chapman and the birth of the 'WM' formation

Chapman was a highly successful manager, gaining major honours at first with Huddersfield Town. He took them from the second division to the first; won the FA Cup in 1922 and two years later claimed the first of a hat-trick of championships for the Yorkshire club, though he moved to Arsenal before his Huddersfield team completed the final one in 1926. At Highbury, he assembled a team of expensive players.

Chapman was a sharp operator and a gifted publicist, with the

1930s appearance of a smartly dressed gangster, spats and all. When he died prematurely in 1934 (just before Arsenal completed a championship treble), he bequeathed a tactical response to the changed offside law that haunted – and still haunts – the game in the country of its birth.

The essence of Chapman's reorganization was to move the centre-half even further back so that he became the 'stopper' between the two full-backs. The defence was further shored-up by the withdrawal of the two inside-forwards into midfield, allowing the wing-halves (half-backs) to concentrate almost entirely on restricting attackers. Thus the famous 'WM' formation came into existence, a 3–2–2–3 tactical shape):

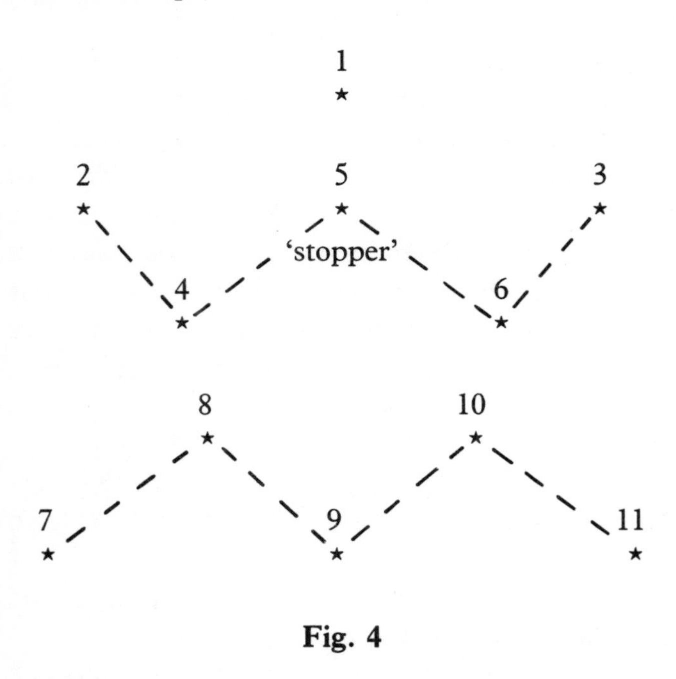

Fig. 4

Within this system, the bulk of the work was performed by the quadrangle of four players in midfield – Nos. 4, 6, 8 and 10 – who did most of the fetching and carrying. Of course, the numbering of some of the players in this new system was now illogical. The No. 5 was really a No. 3, while the left-back should have become the

No. 4, the wing-halves 5 and 6. But somehow the English public never quite saw it like that, not for the next thirty years anyway, and their confusion was compounded by the British insistence on pretending – at least on paper and before a match kicked off – that the No. 5 'stopper' was still a midfield player. Consequently, right up until the 1960s and beyond, match programmes and newspapers in Britain continued to represent players in the (by now ancient) pyramid formation, and the players lined up like that until the whistle blew for kick-off, when they promptly reverted to 3–2–2–3. Amazingly, the British even represented foreign teams (like the Hungarians) as if they played in the same archaic pyramid shape.

In Europe

The English 'WM' formation was not adopted immediately or enthusiastically by the continentals. The archetypal British centre-half – a tall, robust character – had simply to prevent the attacking centre-forward from scoring. Full stop. He had to head the ball away as far as he could when crosses came in from the wings, and otherwise 'get rid of it' as soon as possible. This position was known variously abroad as the 'policeman', 'bodyguard', even in Sweden 'overcoat' because he hung off the shoulders of the opposing No. 9. Somehow the Europeans never quite cottoned on to this role, which is not to say that they could not play a defensive game on the continent; rather the contrary, especially in Switzerland and, later, Italy (where they developed the catenaccio ('bolt') system with a highly defensive 'sweeper'). But the Europeans always expected more football from their centre-halves than the British did after Chapman, and those centre-halves in Britain who liked to play football – like T G Jones at Everton in the post-war period – often lost their places in the team.

Arsenal's phenomenal success with this formation – five championships in eight years and two FA Cups – in the country recognized as the 'home of football' eventually convinced even natural attackers like the Hungarians that what they called 'the defensive centre-half game' should be adopted. By the end of the 1930s it was generally in use (though the Austrian 'Wonder Team' continued to experiment), but the continentals who adopted the 'stopper' often preferred to retain some of the positive elements of the original, play-making role that this once proud centre-forward had occupied many years before.

The Hungarians, however, didn't adopt the new defensive tactic until after a series of lectures about it delivered in Budapest by Arthur Rowe in 1940. Hidegkuti remembers the public debate over the system pioneered by Herbert Chapman:

Hidegkuti: 'We were all reading the sports papers, some of which were reporting very enthusiastically about the English 'WM' formation. One local journalist, Laszlo Feleki, spent months at Highbury dissecting it. In Hungary, arguments broke out all over the place for and against. Some people said it didn't suit the Hungarian style and temperament. The great Ferencvaros striker Gyorgy Sarosi predicted that the game would lose its beauty and become mere semantics. For most of our club teams, it was difficult to find the players to make this system work and confusion reigned for a while. All the strikers were against it.' (Hidegkuti & Fekete, 1965)

By the time Puskas came to make his debut, aged sixteen in 1943, the 'WM' formation was in common use. But within a few years, changes were to take place in Hungary that would mark a new chapter in the modern game; a revolution in tactics and formation that remains with us to the present day.

The Hungarian 'revolution'

Tactics in the real football world, if they are to be of any use at all, are about players. Anyone can play perfect games on a blackboard, but on a pitch, with opponents attempting to disrupt every move, it is those with the ball at their feet who most influence affairs. Even major innovations are often the result of a simple equation: footballing ideas + available players = tactical strategy.

The Hungarians were certainly used to thinking seriously about the game and how it should or could be played. In between the wars, their players gained a reputation as models – almost 'missionaries' – of attacking, skilful, individualistic football. Hungarian coaches were even more prized, and they travelled all over Europe and beyond. One of them, Lajos Czeizler, even became Italy's manager.

The 'deep-lying centre-forward' strategy and 4–2–4

Grosics: In Hungary, a totally different tactical system evolved. It was first introduced at the MTK club where the celebrated trainer Marton Bukovi worked. It was a typically Bukovi idea and he was largely responsible for developing it. (K&S)

Hidegkuti: 'The atmosphere was always great with Bukovi. When we played training matches mid-week, he would play everyone out of position, even ordering attackers to play as defenders and vice-versa. Even in league matches we were encouraged to abandon strict positional roles. The centre-forward was having increasing difficulties with a marker around his neck, and the idea emerged to play the No. 9 deeper where there was some space.'

Vandor: It was Bukovi's idea, but it was Sebes who found the players to perfect it at the national level.

Hidegkuti: The deep-lying centre-forward game was first played at my club, MTK. After a player called Hoffling departed for Belgium, another centre-forward, Palotas, began to drop back into this position with Bukovi's encouragement and he got a lot of goals coming from deep. Sebes tried Palotas in this position in the national team but the player had a heart condition and couldn't run for a whole match. So after the Swiss game *[in September 1952, see Chapter Five]*, when we were 2–0 down and Sebes put me on instead of Palotas and we won 4–2, I played in this position for the national team and that was how we played until 1956.

Szepesi: Bukovi was the first coach to use Hidegkuti as a deep-lying centre-forward. He thought it was much better to have a player advancing from deep, distributing the ball to the strikers, rather than playing a traditional centre-forward with wingers. Sebes's genius was to adapt it for the national team, with Zakarias dropping back into defence and liberating the rest of the midfield – especially Hidegkuti – to attack. (K&S)

The new formation for the Hungarian national team looked like this:

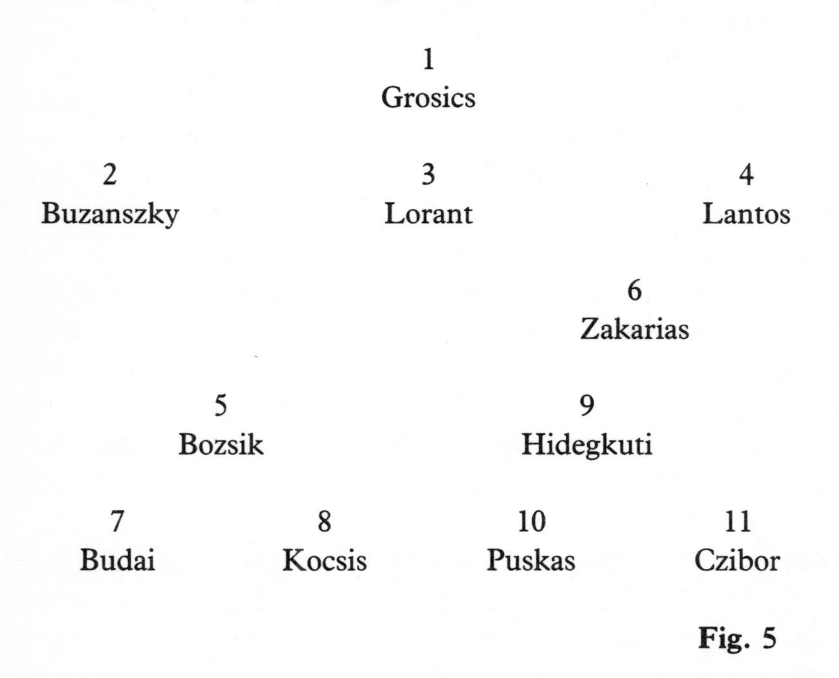

Fig. 5

Grosics: Whoever was in this deep-lying position had to co-ordinate the whole team's strategy from behind the attack. This was the system that Sebes took over from Bukovi and introduced at the national level. We first began to use it in 1950–51, and it was well developed by the time of the Olympics in '52. We soon realized just how revolutionary a tactic it was, because no one else seemed to know about it in advance and, consequently, they all found it very difficult to defend against. If the English gave the world the 'WM' formation, then we can honestly say that it was us who gave the world this new system. Four years later, the Brazilians gave it a name that caught on: the 4–2–4. It was the typical Hungarian tactical shape that became 'typically Brazilian'. (K&S)

The gift to Brazil

The old coach Bela Guttmann, who had briefly managed the Kispest club, was the principal source of transmission of the 4–2–4 system when he worked in Brazil after 1956.

Puskas: Guttmann taught the Brazilians what was a revolutionary tactic for them and brought extra colour to their football. I'm not sure how significant that was in the further development of the game in Brazil but they won three of the next four World Cups, didn't they? They always had brilliant players but they learnt to get the ball forward slowly, with careful passing movements. With Pele, they needed three other strikers to support him; the team was always very well prepared and had great technique, but in the end, regardless of tactics, you've got to have the players that make the tactics work. Anyway, Guttmann was in Brazil for a couple of years and taught them how to play 4–2–4.

Szepesi: The Brazilians like to credit themselves with inventing the 4–2–4 system and indeed they won the World Cup with that formation in 1958. It was an important factor in that victory and they seemed to take many people by surprise with it, but it was the same formation that Hungary used in the early 1950s. Incidentally, it was also the formation used *against* Brazil in the 1954 World Cup when Hungary defeated them in the quarter-final. After the collapse of the Golden Squad side in 1956, the Brazilians took over the development of the 4–2–4 system and perfected it. They formed a much more solid back-four than the Hungarians ever did. That was always the weakest point for us, illustrated by the fact that while the Hungarian forwards scored six at Wembley, the defence conceded three. So the Brazilians played 4–2–4 superbly and evolved it further. That was how they managed to win the World Cup so many times; that and, of course, having the players like Pele, Gerson and Didi who could make it work.

Puskas: The development of the deep-lying centre-forward strategy – the 4–2–4 system with Hidegkuti in the central role – was our masterpiece. He was a great player and a wonderful reader of the game. He was perfect for that role, sitting in forward-midfield, making the telling passes, dragging the opposite defence out of shape and making those fantastic runs himself to score. We had a tremendous understanding of everything required to play the game. Sebes played his part, of course, but it was the players themselves that made it possible.

Hidegkuti: Though all six of us could attack, we never played in a 'line' formation. If I went forward, Puskas dropped back. If Kocsis drifted wide, Bozsik moved into the centre. There was always space to play the ball into. Our right-back Buzanszky advanced down the wing if Budai moved inside. Nobody was expecting a right-back 'overlapping' his winger in those days, so we always had someone free to pass to. Sometimes Czibor would abandon his left wing and join Budai on the right. We constantly changed positions, so where we lined up at kick-off was irrelevant. We concentrated on creating the maximum confusion in our opponents' defence. Our tactics had an enormous impact, not only in Europe where coaches and trainers travelled all over the place to watch us play – and even Hungarian club sides attracted a lot of attention – but also far afield.

Buzanszky: Football, just like everything else in life, is propelled forward by new discoveries. As in chemistry, physics or any field of science, so in football. The way we played was a landmark in the game's development which the Brazilians continued so effectively.

The new goalkeeping role

Grosics: The 'WM' system laid great importance on defence and didn't leave much of an opportunity for a goalie to leave his line and intervene in the game directly. But the new Hungarian style demanded exactly the opposite and I had to adapt to the requirements. Our great strength was our brilliant attackers and a totally offensive game-plan, as you can see just looking at the number of goals we scored. But it did mean that our defence tended to be more loose than many, providing more opportunities for the opposition to counter-attack when they got possession. There was space behind our defence to be exploited and I had to act as a kind of extra 'sweeper', outside of my area, trying to reach the through ball before the opponent did. Sometimes I succeeded; other times I didn't.

I was inspired as a young keeper by a trainer called Peter Szabo who encouraged me to think creatively about the role and to find my own solutions. Rolling the ball out rather than kicking it, for example, was one of the things I developed. It was much more accurate – and quicker – than just hoofing it upfield. You could get the ball straight to your play-makers as well. Once they knew what was happening, Puskas and Hidegkuti learned to drop back to within 25 metres of the area, well within range of a throw.

The crucial roles

Grosics: I watched the team a lot from the back, of course. There was a vital square at the centre of our play, made up of Bozsik, Hidegkuti, Kocsis and Puskas. Those four points defined what was possible on the pitch, and it was their movement and activity that loosened opposing defences to the point where brilliant wingers like Budai and Czibor could prosper. The whole system required a very high level of technical knowledge from those four players, and the rare skill to improvise – something only world-class footballers possess. And make no mistake, they were world-class.

Buzanszky: When a match had kicked off – after about ten or fifteen minutes, say – we could figure out which flank of our opposing team was the weaker; where the vulnerable points in their defence lay. This information was then very quickly processed by our 'computers' – Puskas, Bozsik and Hidegkuti, principally – and they reorganized the tactics to suit the particular occasion. Immediately, the rest of the team responded to any change. We didn't stick rigidly to an initial plan. Our luck was to have such good computers, more powerful and faster than anyone else's.

Sebes: 'Puskas had a brilliant sense of tactical requirements and the ability, in a matter of seconds, to realize what was necessary to surmount a problem, and to solve it quickly. His concentration was acute; it was as if the game took place within a closed room and nothing distracted him: it was just the ball, his team-mates and the opposition. His eye encompassed the whole pitch and his passing revealed his insight. He was never a selfish player, despite his own abilities, and didn't hesitate to lay the ball off to a better-placed colleague. He was the real leader of the team on the pitch, encouraging and driving others on. Most of all, he loved *winning*.'

Puskas: After about five minutes of a match, we could usually work out our opponents' game-plan and adjust accordingly. We didn't get any lengthy pre-match lectures from Sebes, only a brief talk perhaps about one or two of our opponents. If the coach wanted to use very particular tactics, we would talk about that. But we knew exactly who would do what job in the team. If Kocsis advanced, I would drop in behind him; if Czibor wandered on to the right wing, Budai would play deeper, and so on. We played an awful lot of football *without* the ball; it's not just about dribbling and passing. To tell the truth, sometimes with Czibor none of us knew what he would do next, not even himself. But if he decided to spend half the match on Budai's wing, then I would drift wide on the left to compensate.

Szepesi: I loved Hidegkuti, Bozsik and Kocsis, and they were all world-class players. But in my opinion, the all-time greatest Hungarian player is Puskas. He had three unique qualities. For one, he was born a genius. Second, he was a natural captain who prepared for every match very thoroughly – he played the game in his imagination twenty-four hours before it happened. And thirdly, he was such an adorable rascal, a real street urchin, and there aren't many of them around in the whole world, never mind just Hungary.

4

Olympic Champions, 1952

'It was during the Olympics that our football started to flow with real power.'

The year of the Helsinki Olympics marked the high point of the Stalinist dictatorship in Hungary. The general secretary of the Communist Party, Matyas Rakosi, was appointed Prime Minister, and every facet of Hungarian life was rigorously controlled and organized by the regime.

Hungary had not entered the 1950 World Cup in Brazil – probably for financial reasons – but the Olympic Games of 1952 were taken very seriously by the leading Hungarian politicians and the Sports Ministry, as indeed they were amongst all the socialist bloc countries, for whom sport was a major weapon in the propaganda war with the West. With no commercial interests allowed in football in the Eastern bloc, all the players were, if only technically, 'amateurs' and therefore eligible to compete in the Olympics. In addition to the national teams from Eastern Europe there were also some other very good sides, like Sweden and Italy, in the football competition. The English FA, renowned for its insularity, had only entered its first World Cup in 1950 and, because of disagreements over the definition of 'amateurism', did not send a team to Helsinki.

Sebes: 'From the minute it was decided that we would participate in the Olympic Games, I called up the best coaches in Hungary. I wanted Gyula Mandi and also Marton Bukovi to join me on the bench for the Games. It was a bit of a surprise, consequently, when all the competitors and coaches gathered in March for the taking of the oath before a coterie of politicians and sports VIPs, to find that Bukovi was missing. He was not invited. I got a call from Rakosi himself to tell me that Bukovi had been replaced by Jeno Kalmar.

'I was worried about how few international matches were arranged in the lead-up to the Games – two abroad and one in Budapest – and I argued that we needed more but failed to get my way.'

Sebes did have the advantage of being able to fine-tune his tactical plans with the national team on a weekly, sometimes twice-weekly, basis both during regular Honved matches and in the mid-week games when the national team played 'out of town'. Puskas hardly noticed any difference to his usual routine.

Puskas: We travelled a lot in the winter before the Olympic Games, which meant we could play most of the year round. During the cold months when football was suspended in Hungary, we might go on tour to somewhere like Egypt where we could continue to practise in warmer conditions.

Otherwise, in the year prior to the Games, life just went on as usual. I lived at home with my wife Erzebet, and went to Honved or wherever for training in the morning. On a match day, if it wasn't a strong team we were playing, I would travel from my house in Kispest on the number 43 tram to the ground and return the same way. Sometimes, after the Nepstadion was built, we would play big league games there and, of course, any national games. On those occasions we would all assemble at an army facility on Margaret Island *[in the middle of the Danube river, close to the centre of Budapest]* on the Friday evening and return there after the match for dinner together on the Saturday.

The Moscow visit

After the Austrians, the team most ordinary Hungarians wanted to see beaten was the Soviet Union, representing the occupying army in Hungary. But the Golden Squad were somehow never able to defeat the Russians, at least not until a few weeks before the Uprising of 1956. Many Hungarians were convinced that their boys were instructed 'politically' not to beat the Russians, but neither Sebes, Puskas nor any of the other surviving players gives this widely held suspicion any credence (see Chapter 7). The refereeing of these needle matches, though, was another matter.

Sebes: 'At the end of May, we went to Moscow for two 'unofficial' matches. You couldn't call them anything else because there was a Soviet referee on both occasions.* I think a lot of us thought that Hungary v the Soviet Union was a likely Olympic final. There were 100,000 in the Dynamo stadium and our boys were very impressed with the facilities. You could see how the Russians loved their football, but there should have been an impartial ref. We drew the first match 1–1 and didn't play well. There were some good Russian players – Salnikov at right-half and Bobrov up front stood out – but what they were allowed to do was strange. The referees ignored the use of hands to assist jumping or tackling (apparently this was allowed in Soviet league matches) and we just couldn't get used to it.

'I made the players travel by the Moscow underground so they could see for themselves the marble stations and

* These matches are not included in the international record books.

sculptures. Our hosts were very keen on the cultural side of things and arranged long walks for the players around museums (on match days!) and visits to the Bolshoi ballet. I wasn't too keen on the long walks. When I returned home I got a call from the most powerful of our political leaders, Rakosi, to ask why I didn't appreciate the museum trips. Obviously somebody had reported back my remarks. I told him the museums were beautiful, but exhausting.

'The Soviet Union had only just joined FIFA that year. Previously they had no national team – only their clubs travelled abroad – so these were their first 'international' games. We played even worse in the second match and lost 2–1, but the games were very useful; all our imperfections were exposed, particularly at centre-half and in the No. 9 position. I wanted our play to be quicker, and Grosics was a key man here. I wanted him to speed up his throwing or passing of the ball to our defenders, as he tended to dawdle around. During training matches I made him play outfield, at full-back, so he could experience the problem for himself. After Moscow, there were only forty days to go before we left for Helsinki, with still so much to do.'

Preparations for the Olympics

Sebes: 'A month before the Games, we had a match against the Poles in Warsaw. I couldn't go with the team, so I gave the coach a letter to be opened in the dressing-room only minutes before the match kicked off. The contents said simply, "Not Palotas as the No. 9, but Hidegkuti." Apparently it was an embarrassing moment because Palotas already had the shirt on and Hidegkuti was seated in the stands. The thing was, Hidegkuti suffered from terrible nerves before an international match. He was thirty years old, an excellent player, mostly at inside-right for his club, but in that role he lay deep behind the strikers: just what I wanted him to do for the national team in the No. 9 shirt. So I needed to trick him into the match. He played brilliantly and we won 5–1.'

Puskas: Things got really serious about ten days before the Olympic competition. We were sequestered away together and involved in intense training and tactical discussions. We worked on set-pieces and tight passing moves inside the opponents' penalty area. We did gymnastics, sprinting, various games with the ball, and practice matches against other Hungarian teams.

Just before the team set off for Helsinki, Puskas's daughter Aniko was born. The Hungarians generally felt good at the prospect of travelling to Finland, the only other European country with a language related to Hungarian.

Sebes: 'In June we played the Finns in Helsinki as a kind of public relations exercise. I wanted an entertaining, fair game so that the locals would feel well disposed towards us and, if their own team was knocked out, support us. (It paid off, too, in the semi-final against Sweden.) We won 6–1 and returned home with more confidence. Before departing again, we invited the Austria Vienna club to play a couple of games in Budapest. Hidegkuti and Kocsis were in superb form, the latter scoring the first "overhead" goal any of us had ever seen. Even the Austrian players and goalie ran to congratulate Kocsis.'

Olympic matches

Once the Olympic football competition got underway in Finland, Hungary started well, beating Romania 2–1 in a rough, tough game which saw Kocsis sent off in the final minutes. Italy fell next before the emergent 4–2–4 Hungarian system, and Turkey were thrashed 7–1 in the quarter-final. In the semi-final, Hungary met the much-fancied Sweden team and gave them a 6–0 roasting. It was this performance – which some commentators rate as one of the Golden Squad's finest games – which really brought the Hungarian team unmistakably to the world's attention. It was the tactics they adopted, along with their exceptional technique, that caused a great stir, particularly the use of the deep-lying centre-forward strategy.

Puskas: We played like a dream in that semi-final. It must have been very painful for the Swedes to run into us in such form. Losing a semi is bad enough of itself, but 6–0 is a real battering and I felt quite sorry for them. I scored quite soon after kick-off in the match and an early goal always worked well for us, settling us down and allowing us to play our game. It was one of those days. Once we'd hit our rhythm, we were virtually irresistible. Everything we did seemed to come off perfectly. As captain, I didn't try to orchestrate things on the pitch – we knew each other too well to require that – but I screamed a bit if there were passes going astray (and not just when I didn't get the ball, as some people said).

Sebes: 'At the semi, there were thousands of Swedish fans but the Finns supported us. We started well and Puskas scored early. Our attacks were building beautifully but the Swedes didn't panic and came on strong in the second half; I'd never seen them play better. But the subtle shifts of position in our tactical shape confused them; Lorant in the centre of our defence, and Zakarias, were solid; Puskas and the boys up front were magnificent. I felt enormous satisfaction after the match and began to prepare seriously for the final.'

The Wembley match proposed

Among the spectators at the Swedish match was Stanley Rous, along with Gyorgy Szepesi, the Hungarian radio commentator, and Sandor Barcs, then president of the Hungarian FA.

Szepesi: It was a wonderful game. After the match, Stanley Rous of the English FA approaches Sebes and congratulated him with the words: 'Mr Sebes, I think it's time we arranged a match between England and Hungary.'

Barcs: I always say winning at Wembley wasn't as difficult as getting there. At the height of the Stalinist period in Hungary, everything was controlled from the centre. For example, if a foreign FA wrote to us, the letter would not be delivered to me at the Hungarian FA but rather direct to the officials at the Sports Ministry who would translate it, take advice from the Party bosses and instruct us how we should reply.

In 1952, Stanley Rous and I watched Hungary beat Sweden together. That 6–0 victory remains one of the finest performances by any team I've ever seen in my life. After the match Stanley Rous said to me, 'Look, you'll have to come to London and play England soon. Let's shake hands on it.' I played for time, saying I was only the president and would have to consult my executive committee at home. I didn't dare tell him what the real situation was – that neither the FA nor even the Sports Ministry could decide such matters. Only the nation's political leaders could sanction such a match.

I immediately told Sebes and others from the Sports Ministry about the invitation. They were all enthusiastic at the prospect and I wrote a report to the political bosses on my return. Nothing happened for a few months, then the Sports Minister *[Gyula Hegyi]* received a phone call from one of the secretaries of the Central Committee to ask if a victory in London could be guaranteed! Hegyi told the secretary that nothing was certain in football. A few more weeks passed and Sebes got a call with a similar demand. Sebes told me about it and I knew I would get one too, and sure enough, two or three weeks later I did. I said no one could guarantee such a thing in football, but I felt we could guarantee a sensational game with world coverage of the event.

Sebes: 'Towards the end of 1952 there was a meeting of European FA leaders in Switzerland, attended by myself and Stanley Rous. He officially proposed the Wembley match then, to mark the ninetieth anniversary of the Football Association. *[In fact, the England v Rest of the World match – a 4–4 draw – played on 21 October, 1953 at Wembley, was the official match to mark the anniversary.] I was delighted and shook hands with him. I travelled back to Budapest by train but Stanley Rous flew home to London and announced on his arrival that England would play Hungary at Wembley on 25 November 1953. By the time I got home, there were already reports in the media of the forthcoming match and I got carpeted by the Prime Minister and Party boss, Rakosi. He was very annoyed at first, insisting that the game had not yet been officially sanctioned. I managed to persuade him that even if we lost, it would be an historic occasion. I told him no foreign football team had ever left Wembley victorious, but in football nothing was for ever.'*

The Olympic Final: Hungary 2 Yugoslavia 0

Football had been developing fast in Belgrade and the Yugoslavs were a strong, skilful team, tactically astute and well able to test the resilience of a Hungarian team of whom much was now expected, and whose nerves were beginning to fray a little at the edges. It wasn't only the players who were feeling the pressure: political relations between Hungary and Yugoslavia were also getting strained.

Sebes: 'I could see the tension on the faces of our players at the tactical talk we had on the morning of the Final. To Puskas and Czibor, I underlined the danger posed by their best player, Cajkovski, but I mentioned nothing about the phone call I'd received from Rakosi, back home. He rang to tell me that failure would not be tolerated. It was not permitted to lose!'

Puskas: The Yugoslavs were a good outfit but we outplayed them on the day. I missed a penalty. I was not too happy, I can tell you, I haven't missed many in my career and that was a painful one. I changed my mind on the run-up. I thought I was going to fool the goalie, but he fooled me. Instead of going for the left-hand corner, I switched to the right and he got across to hold it. I felt like kicking myself but it didn't last long.* In the second half we relaxed a bit – we were very tense in such a big match at first – and the goals came. I got one and Czibor the other. I was a real bogeyman for the Yugoslavs. They never beat us once when I was playing for Hungary, not between 1946 and 1956. They did win once in Budapest after the '56 Uprising, but of course I had gone by then.

Sebes: 'The Olympics demonstrated our growing strength in defence and the ability of all five of our attackers to score goals. Teams now knew it wasn't just Puskas and Kocsis they had to watch. But while the international press were full of praise for us, at home the papers were emphasizing that the world's best teams weren't at the Games in Finland. But I knew we could get better, fitter and faster. I warned the players that there was more hard work ahead.'

Puskas: Much of the credit for our success must go to Gusztav Sebes and his assistant Gyula Mandi for their dedication and footballing genius. They were always with us in training and everywhere we went, taking good care of us and doing everything they could to get us in the right condition. They helped foster an enormous loyalty amongst us all. Even after we had been unbeaten for years, we always gave our best for them, continuing to try to excel; running that bit quicker, jumping that bit higher, striking the ball that much more accurately. It was during the

* According to Sebes, Puskas felt so badly about this miss that he spent the next few minutes diving around in the penalty box trying to win another spot-kick.

Olympics that our football first started to flow with real power. It was a proto-type of 'total football': when we attacked, everyone attacked; in defence, it was just the same.

Sebes: 'To their credit, the Yugoslavian press were generous in defeat (something I'm sure the Hungarians would never have been) but when I attended a reception at their Budapest embassy, I was the only one of our sports leaders there. That was typical.'

The homecoming

It had been another very successful Olympic Games all round for Hungary. In addition to the football gold medal, the nation won a further 15 golds to take third place in the overall medals table behind the USA and the Soviet Union, a remarkable achievement for such a small nation and a testament to both the native Hungarian talent and the political commitment of the state to producing sporting excellence. Victories for Hungarian sportsmen and women also gave the people at home a rare opportunity to celebrate Hungarian national identity and culture, something which the political realities often made it difficult for them to express. For many in Hungary, the national football team provided one brief, but increasingly reliable, interlude of joy – and pride – during a veritable reign of state terror.

Puskas: It was a great trip home from Helsinki by train with all the other athletes, so many of whom had done so well against the best in the world. After we left Prague, heading for the Hungarian border, the train was stopping ever more frequently to allow the crowds to greet us as we passed through stations. The scenes at Keleti station in Budapest were unbelievable. There were around 100,000 folks jammed in the surrounding streets to celebrate. The Party officials were out in force, of course, and there was much speechifying from makeshift platforms and great applause when we showed our faces. We were almost ecstatic, such joy welling up. This was our first great victory and our hearts were still so young.

5

England versus Hungary

'I would say 1953 is still my favourite year.'

In March 1953, Stalin died. Following the old Soviet dictator's death, crowds of workers in East Berlin staged violent demonstrations and protests. At the start of June, 20,000 Hungarian workers from the huge Rakosi iron and steel works in Budapest, named after the Hungarian dictator, downed tools in protest at low wages and poor conditions. Other strikes broke out in eastern Hungary and peasant demonstrations were organized on the great Hungarian plains. Within weeks, the leaders of the Hungarian Communist Party, including Matyas Rakosi and Mihaly Farkas, together with Imre Nagy, were summoned to Moscow by Khrushchev and the new Soviet leaders. Rakosi was severely cricitized for allowing affairs in Hungary to reach such a head, and the almost immediate outcome was the reorganization of the Party in the spirit of 'collective leadership'.

The Hungarian Central Committee quickly published resolutions criticizing the former policies of the regime and in July, Nagy replaced Rakosi as Prime Minister and announced his government's 'New Course' programme, which included amnesties for political prisoners and the abolition of internment camps as well as other economic and social reforms. Rakosi, however, was merely demoted and remained First Party Secretary. It was against this background of rising hope and expectation that the Hungarian Golden Squad hit their most sustained and brilliant form.

The build-up to the Wembley game

Sebes: 'There was little rest for the players after the Olympics. The league started in August, and in September we played the Swiss in Berne. It was a very significant match because it was our first as Olympic champions, and it decided once and for all the player best suited to the deep-lying No. 9 role.

'Palotas had played very well during the Olympics, so I played him and dropped Hidegkuti to the subs' bench. In front of 35,000 Swiss fans, the home team went two-up within half an hour and I sent Hidegkuti on for Palotas a few minutes later. The transformation was amazing. He seemed to complement the partnership between Puskas and Kocsis perfectly, and beautiful passes began to flow amongst the three of them. Before half-time, Hidegkuti had laid two goals on for Puskas and we were on level terms.

'I tried to explain to them at the break what had caused the problems in the first half-hour. The Swiss were getting all their men behind the ball and drawing our defenders into risky attacks. Everyone in our team wanted to score, and we were exposed to counter-strikes. I told our lads to keep the ball more in midfield and loosen the Swiss defence before trying to penetrate it. They did it to perfection in the second half, with Bozsik and Hidegkuti arriving late to add to their confusion. We won 4–2 and beat Czechoslovakia 5–0 in the final match of 1952. It was a good year: played 10, won 10, scored 45 goals, conceded only 6.'

Rome, 1953: Italy 0 Hungary 3

Hungary were on a roll: they played six more matches before

November 1953 – five of them away – and were now unbeaten in three years, with 19 wins in 22 matches, including a famous 3–0 victory over Italy in Rome in May of that year.

Sebes: 'In the 1920s, quite few good Hungarian players and coaches had gone to work in Italy and, though Hungarian football languished, the Italians improved enormously and won two World Cups *[1934 and 1938]*. They love their football, of course, and as we were crossing the border by train before the Rome match, the Italian railworkers learned who was in the carriages and insisted on showing us their new train engine. Next thing, Puskas is driving it off down the track.

'The match in Rome, which inaugurated the new Olympic Stadium, was a big game. I'd learnt a lot, tactically, from that match against the Swiss when we had gone two goals down so quickly, so I kept the defence much tighter and asked for attacks to be launched from midfield. I played Hidegkuti even though he was only half-fit, because I needed his fine technique and tactical guile to penetrate the world's toughest defence. We hadn't beaten the Italians in twenty-eight years, but this time it was different. Puskas got two and Hidegkuti one.'

It was a magnificent performance from the Hungarians. Throughout the match they were so hungry for goals; a simple victory was clearly not enough for them. In his live radio commentary from Rome, Szepesi describes how Puskas is screaming for the ball from Grosics. He doesn't want his goalkeeper to hold the ball for a moment longer than necessary. Despite being away from home and two-nil up with only twenty minutes to go, Puskas is still urging attack at every opportunity. At the end, even the Italian fans are applauding the visitors.

In recordings of the post-match radio interviews in the dressing-room, you can hear the joy in the voices of the Hungarian players. Winning the Olympics in Helsinki is one thing; beating Italy 3–0 in Rome is another. They can hardly credit their own achievement. In his interview, Puskas, however, is wise enough to credit 'the authorities' for allowing the team to prepare so thoroughly for this great match. The team captain was no fool.

Sebes: 'The Italian press were full of our praises after the match, talking about the new form of attacking football we were demonstrating. I didn't normally get so tactically involved with preparations for a game – only for the really important ones – and could usually leave it up to the team to sort things out. But this was a fine performance, using short balls to draw out the Italian defence and then hitting long ones wide to get round the back of them.'

The Hungarians had some very good young players coming through as well, illustrated by their success in the European Junior Championship in spring 1953 when they didn't concede a goal in the whole competition. The Golden Squad continued to carry all before them, defeating Czechoslovakia 5–1 in Prague on 4 October and Austria 3–2 in Vienna a week later. But Sebes was beginning to have one or two problems with some of his star players.

Sebes: 'I'd learned that Budai, Kocsis and Czibor had all been out all night on a bender, straight after training, late in September. So I left all three of them out against Czechoslovakia – a bit of a risk, as they were immensely popular – despite criticism in the papers. Anyway, we won easily. I played Budai in Vienna because I had since heard that he had gone home at midnight, but the other two were still in my bad books. Finally, I went to see them individually at home and gave them my thoughts about the way a sportsman should behave and look after himself. I told them that I wanted them to play at Wembley, and that if we beat the English there our names would be legendary. They promised to reform and give of their best. From that day, I only had one thing on my mind: the Wembley match.

'I had visited Wembley to see England play the Rest of Europe *[a 4–4 draw]* a few weeks earlier, and the day after the match I returned to the stadium, put my boots on and tried out the famous turf. I noticed that even high balls didn't bounce more than a metre. I measured the pitch and tried to work out where the sun would be on the afternoon of our match. I also asked Stanley Rous if I might have a match ball to take home with me and he graciously gave me three. Back in Budapest, I chose a pitch with the nearest measurements I could find to Wembley and we trained there with Stanley's match balls, three times a week from early November, playing teams imitating the typical English formation.'

Buzanszky: The English balls were very different. When we first kicked them, it felt as if you were kicking something made of wood. Our balls were softer, more sensitive. So we tried to get used to the English ones.

The prelude

On 15 November 1953, ten days before the Wembley match, Hungary faced Sweden (whom they had beaten so emphatically in Helsinki) in the Nepstadion in Budapest. They did not produce the best performance to give confidence before meeting England.

Sebes: 'I nearly forgot about the match with Sweden, and didn't prepare for it properly at all. We played with an English ball, and the players hadn't had enough time to get used to it (though the Swedes had no problems). My lads wanted the ball to be changed at half-time but I wasn't having any of that. Everyone was desperate not to be injured; Puskas even missed a penalty, it was awful. But I was glad in one way. The English FA had sent a party of seven coaches and analysts to watch the match, and at least I knew they had seen nothing of the tactics I intended to use at Wembley.'

Puskas: We played terribly against the Swedes. I missed a penalty and hit the post, and Hamrin headed the equalizer in the last minute. We got well and truly sorted out by the fans and the press after this draw. They were saying, 'It's not worth you going over to Wembley if you can't do better than that. The English are a serious football team, unbeaten for ninety years at home, they'll murder you.' We kept our cool and told the journalists: 'Don't worry about us, just look after the writing. We'll play the football and carry the can if necessary.'

Without television in Hungary, most people depended entirely on radio coverage for immediate news of football matches. Commentator Szepesi followed the national team everywhere and was becoming almost as well known in Hungary as the players.

Szepesi: I was sure we would win against England and I can prove it. If you look at the Hungarian *Radio Times* for that week, there was only one match we had scheduled to broadcast twice on the same day – and that was organized three weeks beforehand. The Wembley game was to be covered live in the afternoon, and the whole match repeated at eight o'clock in the evening. As head of the sports desk, it was me who insisted on this because I was convinced that we would take our revenge for that 6–2 defeat in England in 1936.

Sebes: 'We were pilloried in the Hungarian press after the Sweden match. Only families and friends came to see us off at the station for England. My mind went back to Hungary's last game with England in 1936, when we had lost 6–2. I thought through the mistakes we had made in that match and determined we wouldn't make the same mess of it.

'I had written earlier to friends in Paris, where we would stop en route. There was even a small crowd to greet us, which boosted the team's spirits a bit. An amazing 15,000 turned out for a practice match I'd arranged with the Renault factory team and they gave us a standing ovation, which was wonderful to see.'

Puskas: We stopped in Paris for a few days on the way to London and played the Renault car company team where Sebes had worked before the war. We won easily, of course, and scored thirteen goals in the game, and it really did help to get the taste of that bad match with Sweden out of our mouths. Our whole attitude had changed before we arrived in London.

Sebes: 'Everyone was fit, only Grosics was complaining of a sinus infection but I wasn't too worried about that because I knew how he suffered from terrible nerves before a big game and often became hypochondriacal. We were met in London by Stanley Rous. We stayed at the Cumberland Hotel and, fortunately, found a Czech restaurant with a Hungarian cook just round the corner, where we ate all our meals. I planned all the menus in consultation with the team doctor. Loads of telegrams began to arrive from home, wishing us well, and it all helped to lift the mood and prepare the players for the game of their lives. We took a suitcase full of these good wishes with us to Wembley for the match.'

Puskas: We were a bit surprised that we weren't allowed to train at least once on the Wembley pitch which we had heard so much about. We went on to the pitch with our shoes on and it seemed very soft and springy, but that was only our brief first impression. We were allowed to train at QPR's ground *[Loftus Road]* which felt as if it was in the countryside.

Sebes knew that the English were particularly resolute defenders, so he looked for something to upset them tactically. That's why we played the game we did at Wembley. It was one of a variety of options we might have used.

The tactics

Sebes: 'We talked over tactics before the game. I wanted the opposite of the approach we had used against the Italians in Rome. I wanted the main accent on attack, using the four forwards plus Hidegkuti in a swirl of positional fluidity that would utterly confuse the English defence. Our defence had Lorant as sweeper, behind Buzanszky and Lantos, with Zakarias between them, withdrawn from a midfield where Bozsik operated in tandem with Hidegkuti. I wanted the wingers, Budai and Czibor, to drop back when necessary to assist in defence, and Puskas, Kocsis and Hidegkuti all over the place because I thought the English defenders would feel strictly obliged to follow them. As they drew their men, Bozsik would advance into the gap. That was the plan, anyway.'

This is the tactical diagram for the Wembley game reproduced in Sebes's book:

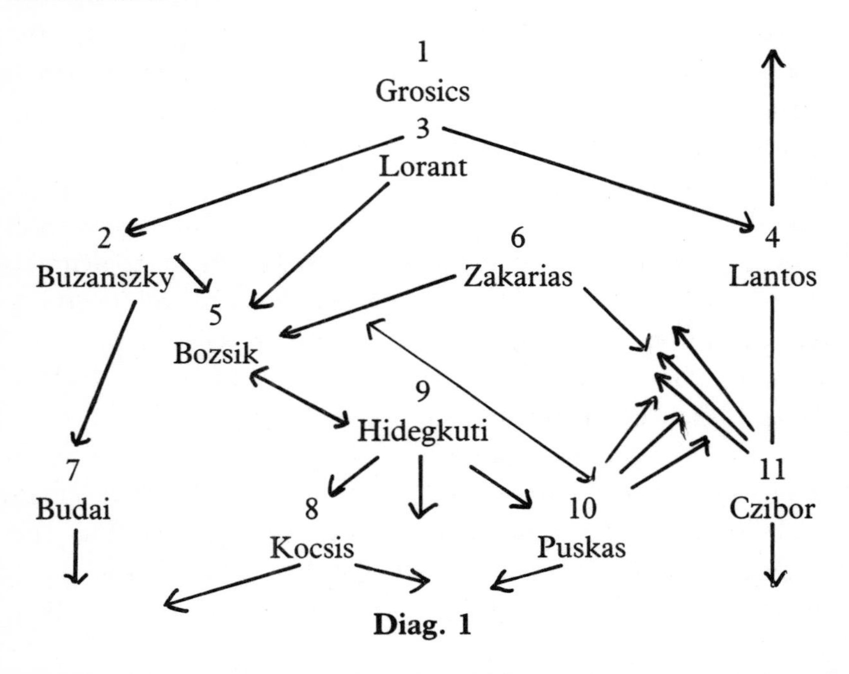

Diag. 1

Barcs: The tactical discussion before the Wembley match lasted about four hours. It took place in the Cumberland Hotel. Sebes spoke for ages and I could understand hardly anything of it. He was so excited, he wasn't making much sense, and I noticed worried expressions on the faces of some of the players.

Buzanszky: We went to Wembley by coach and someone even sang our national anthem en route. Others were singing Hungarian folk songs or doing anything to try and relax. No one chatted and there was an incredible tension in the air.

Grosics: One could almost feel the fear and concern amongst us, and the huge weight of expectation upon us. English football was the best in the world. I think anyone would have been afraid.

Walter Winterbottom was the England manager.

Winterbottom: I think we believed we were good at the game, let's be fair. Everybody expected us still to win on our own soil. Nobody could beat us at Wembley, you know, and all this sort of thing. (K&S)

*England lined up in their traditional 3–2–2–3 formation (***Diag. 2***), known as the 'WM'. In this tactical system, the four players who formed a square in midfield did almost all the work up and down the pitch. The Hungarians called them 'the piano-carriers'.*

England 3 Hungary 6

Buzanszky: If you look at the film of the match, you can see the tension on Puskas's face as he exchanges pennants with Billy Wright before kick-off. But soon it was the English who looked the most distracted.

Puskas: I would be a liar if I said we were not pretty nervous on the day of the match. Everyone was a bit edgy, but it soon passed once we got on to the pitch. We were doing our best to have a

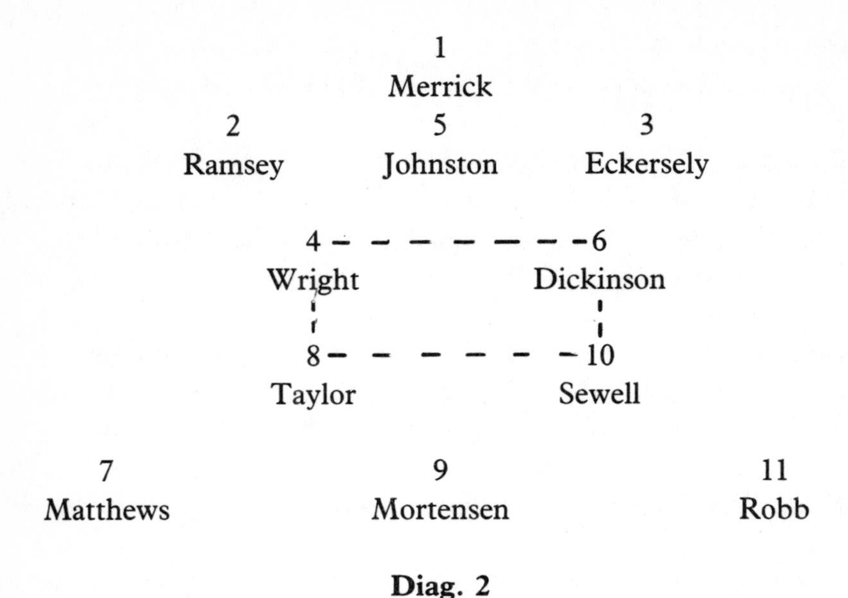

Diag. 2

laugh and forget about the importance of the game. I was in my kit, hanging about in the corridor, when I saw the England inside-right Taylor, who wasn't very tall. I popped back into our dressing-room and said to the others, 'Listen, we're going to be all right, they've got someone even smaller than me.' It broke the tension but we were glad to get out there and kick a ball around to ease our minds.

Buzanszky: We were cautious. We didn't know the English players because the Western press didn't reach further than the Austro-Hungarian border. The cultural attaché at the Embassy in London had done his best to inform Sebes about the players we might face, but we had no idea how much the cultural attaché knew about football. We tried to snatch a look at our individual opponents in the dressing-room area. Luckily, in those days the number a player wore usually indicated the position he played. I didn't know this guy Robb *[England's left-winger, replacing the injured Finney]* but maybe the English players didn't know him either as it was his first time in the England team. So I was stealing glances at him. You can learn a lot by looking at a player's physique. When I saw him, the adrenalin started to pump. I bet my pulse was up around 180 during the warm-up.

England's captain that day was the Wolves half-back, Billy Wright. Like most other Englishmen, he fully expected his team to brush aside the Hungarian challenge.

Wright: Looking back, we completely underestimated the advances that the Hungarians had made, and not only tactically. Do you know, when we walked out at Wembley that Wednesday afternoon, side by side with the visiting team, I looked down and noticed that the Hungarians had on these strange, lightweight boots, cut away like slippers under the ankle-bone. I turned my head over my shoulder to big Stan Mortensen, our No. 9 somewhere behind me, and uttered the immortal words: 'We should be all right here, Stan, they haven't got the proper kit.' It's true, I did.

The Hungarians were ahead within fifty seconds. Bozsik released Hidegkuti in midfield to advance, feint and shoot past Merrick from the edge of the penalty area. Don Howe, currently Technical Co-ordinator with the Football Association, remembers the shock well.

Howe: They murdered us, not only with technical ability but tactics as well. They had Hidegkuti, the centre-forward – well, he did have a number nine on his back – playing from deep midfield. Our centre-half that day, Harry Johnston, didn't know what to do.

Johnston: 'I was in the middle of that first Hungarian Hurricane at Wembley. And to me, the tragedy was the utter helplessness, at times, of being unable to do anything to alter the grim outlook.' (Johnston, 1954, p.49)

England drew level before the quarter-hour, with a swift counter-attack. It was Johnston who began the move after intercepting in his own penalty area. He advanced upfield and found Mortensen, who intelligently played Sewell in to run and shoot past Grosics. But moments before, in one of the most fluent and stunning moves of the whole match, Czibor, Puskas and finally Hidegkuti had combined to produce a wonderful goal that the referee, Leo Horn from Holland, mysteriously disallowed. It made little difference. Within the half-hour, Hungary were 4–1 up. Hidegkuti got their second, in combination with Puskas, Czibor and Kocsis whose clever flick allowed the No. 9 to score from close range. A deflected Bozsik free-kick accounted for the fourth but, minutes before it, Puskas had got the third; the goal that instantly conferred on him footballing immortality.

Puskas: I think my favourite goal of all time was that third one – the 'drag-back'. Everybody thought it was a well-rehearsed move on my part, but it wasn't. It was simply a reflex movement. I was on the right of the goal, at the edge of the six-yard box, when I received the ball from Czibor on the right wing. I had my back to the goal and had to turn, but I saw Billy Wright on his way with an enormous lunging tackle, hurling himself at the ball. He was expecting me to turn inside, and if I had done he would have taken me and the ball off the pitch and into the stands. So I dragged the ball back with the studs of my left boot and whacked it high into the net on the near side of the goalkeeper, where he didn't expect it.

Wright: 'Puskas, the incomparable Puskas, suddenly bobbed up in front of me with the ball. I moved into the tackle firmly, quickly and with my eyes on the ball. Nine times out of ten that tackle would have won possession. But this was the tenth time, and my opponent was Puskas. He dragged the ball back with his studs and my striking leg met . . . just air. In the same incredibly quick movement, the great Hungarian pivoted, his left foot flashed, and there was the ball nestling cosily in the back of the net.' (Green, 1974, p.285)

Puskas: I don't really know where that goal came from. The 'drag-back' was something I used to do as a kid but it wasn't something I'd ever practised. It was instinctive. My football wasn't full of fancy tricks. I liked simple things on the pitch, simple solutions, quick easy movements. Everyone loved the goal – it's probably the one I am best remembered for – but the truth is I had to get out of the way quick, otherwise Billy Wright would have really clobbered me.

The goal was simply stunning, and not only in execution. The whole movement which led to it illustrated the revolutionary fluidity which allowed the Hungarian attackers maximum freedom. Kocsis (the centre-forward with a No. 8 on his shirt) picks up the ball from deep and passes to Czibor (the left-winger) who is overlapping Budai (the right-winger) on Budai's flank. Czibor crosses the ball along the ground for Puskas (the inside-left), who has taken up a position on the right-hand side of the six-yard box, to evade Wright's tackle and score.

If you examine the film of this goal closely, frame by frame, you notice that Puskas's first touch as he receives the ball from Czibor is less than perfect, otherwise Wright would probably have had no opportunity to tackle him at all. The ball drifts away from Puskas towards the dead-ball line, so the necessity for the drag-back and the opportunity to make a tackle both occur at the same moment. But Puskas is faster, both physically and mentally, than the great England captain who is marking him.

Half-time

At half-time the score stood at 4–2, Mortensen having got England's second a few minutes before the break. England's right-winger Stanley Matthews remembers Johnston's confusion about how to deal with Hidegkuti:

Matthews: Harry said to me at half-time, walking to the dressing-room, 'I don't know what to do. Do I go with him, or stay?' You see, we didn't know they had Hidegkuti playing deep. Now when you've got a skilful player playing deep, and no one's marking him, he's gonna kill you. It doesn't mean that if we had marked him we'd have won; but the way it was, we had no chance. (K&S)

Sebes: 'When they came in for half-time I told them they were playing well, but I also told them to remember that the English would never give up, it wasn't their style.'

Puskas: At half-time, we were saying to each other, 'Come on, we've got them, let's just relax and carry on playing.' We told Grosics, 'If you let any more in, we'll give you a good hiding.' The mood was really good. Of course, that first goal from Hidegkuti inside the opening minute was crucial. It came on the end of a five-pass move and gave us a fantastic feeling of confidence. It let us relax and play, and in that mood we were as good as any team in the world. If we were nervous before the game kicked off, so were the English. They watched us juggling the ball in the warm-up (which was the kind of thing we always did before a game) and looked apprehensive, but that first goal put the wind up them.

Groscis: It was a bit of a surprise that England were so unaware of our deep-lying centre-forward strategy. We had been playing it for some time and their coaches must have seen us. But once the game started, it was even more of a surprise that their defence seemed so totally unable to adjust to it once it was apparent. They just kept on playing the same way and that meant that England's centre-half, Johnston, had no-one to mark and didn't know what to do. It also meant that Hidegkuti was free to operate, and score, from midfield.

Wright: It wasn't Puskas that did us. It was Nandor Hidegkuti. We didn't pick him up and he was the creator, he made space. I'm not saying Puskas wasn't the great player he was, but it was the system of playing Nandor deep that pulled us about. We discussed it at half-time, but by then they were four goals to the good. We came better in the second half, but they still had the great individual players. Bozsik, the right-half, was a brilliant attacking player; Czibor and Budai foraging on the flanks, and then Kocsis, a brilliant header of the ball. They were not a bad side!

Winterbottom: This idea that half-time discussion resolves anything, and the manager has only to get stuck in and tell the players to pull their socks up, is a load of nonsense. Players are worried enough without you pouring a lot of abuse on them. Tactics-wise, the Hungarians had it all. They knew just exactly what they were about and they had five of what I would call world-class internationals in that side – Czibor, Bozsik, Hidegkuti, Puskas and Kocsis. World-class players, all of them.

Hidegkuti: Neither the English nor any of the other teams we met seemed able to defend effectively against our tactical formation. If both Bozsik and I joined the attack, we had six strikers advancing, all capable of scoring goals. We used to joke with our defenders sometimes: 'Don't worry if you let one in, we'll score two.' That's how we felt. (K&S)

The second half

The match was as good as over within ten minutes of the restart. Merrick pushed a Czibor header on to the post, but the ball came out to Bozsik just outside the England penalty area. His rising shot was in the net before Merrick blinked. The Hungarians' final goal was volleyed home from an angle after Puskas found Hidegkuti with a wonderful lob. Ramsey got England's third from the penalty spot when Mortensen was brought down. The following morning,

Geoffrey Green of The Times *summed up the afternoon's match for the English:*

'They found themselves strangers in a strange world, a world of flitting red spirits, for such did the Hungarians seem as they moved at devastating pace with superb skill and powerful finish in their cherry bright shirts. One has talked about the new conception of football as developed by the continentals and South Americans. Always the main criticism against the style has been its lack of a final punch near goal. One has thought at times, too, that perhaps the perfection of football was to be found somewhere between the hard-hitting, open British method and this other, more probing infiltration. Yesterday, the Hungarians, with perfect team work, demonstrated this mid point to perfection.'

The match statistics illustrate how aggressively the Hungarians attacked:

	Shots on goal	**Shots on target**	**Corners**	**Goals**
England	**5**	**5**	**3**	**3**
Hungary	**35**	**21**	**6**	**5**

Szepesi: After the match was over, I walked on to the pitch to stand on the spot where Puskas scored that unforgettable goal. As I stood there, I was thinking that after an historic battle they usually erect a memorial. They should place one here where Puskas scored the goal that beat England for the first time.

Matthews: They are the best team I ever played against. That wonderful Hungarian team. Oh, Puskas, Hidegkuti and those fantastic team-mates. They were the best ever. (K&S)

The injured Tom Finney watched the game from the press box, though he would play in the return game in Budapest the following year.

Finney: I still think they were the greatest national side I played against; a wonderful team to watch, with tactics we'd never seen before. It was like cart-horses playing race-horses, and when you think we had people like Stanley Matthews and Stan Mortensen in that game, some great players – but we were just torn asunder. (K&S)

David Barr was one of the 100,000 fans at Wembley that afternoon.

Barr: I didn't know anything about Hungary, but we knew we would win against these impoverished people quite easily. We saw the most magnificent display of football I'll ever see. It was superb. After they'd got their fourth, we no longer minded whether England scored, they were so good. It's something I'll remember all my life. Magnificent men like Puskas and Hidegkuti, so much better than anyone we had. (K&S)

Barcs: The football the English played was full of industry; ours was pure art.

Puskas: I suppose the primary feeling immediately after the match was surprise and pleasure, especially at the thought of all those journalists back home who were presumably busy eating their words. It wasn't easy beating the English for the first time at Wembley. That match took an enormous amount out of all of us. Telegrams began to arrive from all over the world.

Sebes: 'There was a grand reception after the match and I asked the English FA to invite the great old coach Jimmy Hogan to come along. Jimmy was the coach of MTK in Budapest back in the 1920s, and he had done much to raise the standard of Hungarian football in those days. He was getting on a bit, but he came to see us all. The old master told me: "That was the kind of football today that I dreamed the Hungarians might one day be able to play." '

Szepesi: The following morning, there was an interesting encounter at the Cumberland Hotel where the Hungarian party were staying. Stanley Rous arrived and I joined him and Sebes for coffee in a private reception room. The two of them were talking about a return match to be arranged in Budapest when suddenly Mr Rous opened this rather large suitcase he had beside him and said: 'Mr Sebes, I would like to pay you for the wonderful game yesterday at Wembley. How much of the takings would you like?' Sebes looked astonished and waved the money away, but Stanley Rous continued: 'I repeat, gentlemen, I have brought you money, pounds sterling, for yesterday's match.' Sebes wouldn't accept a penny: 'Thank you very much, but we don't want any payment. I am grateful if you can play a return match in Budapest. That is enough.'

Meanwhile, back in Hungary ...

The match with England – relayed via Szepesi's live radio commentary – almost brought Hungary to a standstill for a few hours that Wednesday afternoon. There had been endless pre-match debate about the English weather, the English ball, the texture and dimensions of the Wembley pitch, Puskas and Wright, Merrick and Grosics, Bozsik and Sewell. The whole nation seemed completely absorbed in the prospective game.

On the day of the match, electrical retailers did brisk trade in loudspeakers and radio amplifiers as big stores, restaurants and shops provided continuous coverage for their staff and customers, advertised by notices outside their premises which proudly announced: 'We are broadcasting the Match of the Century.'

At kick-off time – 2.15pm in England – the streets of Budapest were virtually deserted, apart from a few places where people gathered in public around a loudspeaker. Cinemas showed films to empty auditoriums; buses and trams stopped with no passengers aboard. Shift times in factories were rearranged to finish early. In the mines, the score was relayed to the coal-face workers, chalked on the side of the cages which descended the shafts.

Within minutes of the game's conclusion, special editions of the Nepsport *newspaper appeared on the streets. Eight thousand telegrams of congratulation were sent to the victorious team from Budapest alone. The Hungarians took to the streets in crowds to celebrate their joy, and the spell lingered for days afterwards.*

Returning in triumph

In Europe the Hungarian victory was hailed by all, as if it were a general vindication of continental football's progress.

Puskas: When we got to Paris, where we had to change to another railway station, the reception was unbelievable. It was almost as if they themselves had won.

Szepesi: We stayed in a fantastically elegant place, the Hotel Louvre. We also played another match in honour of the coach, Gusztav Sebes. We won 16–1 and the whole of Paris applauded us. It had been like that all the way from Wembley, where the crowd had cheered us from the terraces. The English had cheered us off from Victoria station as well. They are unforgettable memories.

Hidegkuti: We were allowed to stay in Paris for two days, which at the time was a rare treat. We went to a match – Paris v Cannes, I think – and when the crowd learnt we were there they began to shout for us to go on the pitch before the game started, which we did. Some of the crowd wanted the original match abandoned and us to play one half against both teams! When we played the friendly match the next day, the little stadium we were in only held 5,000. Well, there were 10,000 inside that day and another 10,000 outside trying to get in. It was unbelievable.

Szepesi: On our arrival in Paris at the Gare de l'Est, a famous Hungarian banker, Andre Kosztolanyi, was amongst the crowd to greet us. He took us to the Lido – the wonder of Paris at the time – and later we went to the Follies show where the audience were calling out the names of some of the players, Puskas and others. They all ended up on stage to take a bow. It was the same all the way home across Europe. There were crowds of people waiting everywhere the train stopped. Even when we only passed through, the station master waved his congratulations. At the West Bahnhof station in Vienna, the crowd seemed larger than even Paris. Of course there were many Hungarians living there, but thousands of Austrians turned out including the Austrian national team and all the media.

But it was as nothing compared to what was to greet us in Hungary itself. From the border, people simply lined the track, standing guard as the train went past – and remember, this was late November, in cold and wintry conditions.

The little station at Hegyeshalom on the frontier was overwhelmed with locals, and others who had travelled from Budapest to be amongst the first Hungarians to welcome the team on home soil. The national anthem was played as the train pulled in. Players' names were chanted from the platform, as wives and families of the Golden Squad joined the party on board. In Gyor, Komarom, Tatabanya, wherever the train stopped, showers of flowers and gifts descended on the national footballing heroes. Fans tried to delay the train's departure to remain longer with the men who had at last showed the world what Hungarian football could do. The regime, too, did its best to show appropriate gratitude.

Szepesi: My salary as a radio commentator was 2,175 forints at the time. This was quite good money, and at that time Puskas's salary was 4,000. The players' bonus after the Wembley match was exactly the same as mine – a radio commentator! – about 2,000 forints each. Then later, when it became clear what a wonderful victory it had been and that it was being celebrated all over the world, they raised the players' bonuses. Puskas eventually got somewhere between 50–100,000 forints, I think. But all those players earned much less than people thought they did.

Grosics: To understand what a victory like this meant to the Hungarian people, you have to understand what had happened in Hungary since 1949. We lived under a very radical regime that used many weapons, including intimidation, to impose its vision. It included attempting to undermine our national identity and our sense of ourselves. Overtly patriotic works of art were prohibited, for example.

Yet, paradoxically, the state was very keen to push sport as a way of advertising to the world the success of the communist system, and the emergence of the Golden Squad was a part of that. Ironically, our victories made it possible for ten million Hungarians to regain and celebrate their 'Hungarian-ness' in a way the state could hardly disapprove of. While the political authorities tried to monopolize and manipulate our success for their own ends, the mass of people were liberated by the ninety minutes of football: they knew where they belonged and that their souls were Hungarian.

Hidegkuti: The victory at Wembley made the West recognize us, not just in a footballing way. As a small, satellite state of the Soviet empire, we were largely ignored. If our embassies organized something, no one of any importance bothered to come along. But after the 6–3 match, even the Americans sent people. It was full houses in the embassies! An ambassador told us it had never happened before. We also got a lot of invitations to travel abroad to play. And it was all because we'd beaten the English on their own patch. If we'd stuffed the French in Paris, for example, no one would have turned a hair.

The Budapest reception

The Hungarian government pulled out all the stops to welcome the footballers home to the capital. Delegates of the Party, mass workers' organizations, the Young Pioneers, all turned out to celebrate and congratulate the victors.

Szepesi: At Keleti railway station, people were hanging from the trees and dangling from the roofs. The players had to parade down the main street of Budapest so the crowd could properly celebrate them.

Puskas: In Budapest, of course, the reception was stunning. Over 100,000 people milling round Keleti station; Party officials and sports leaders making speeches. It was a national celebration and, though we were all very tired and longed to get home after the journey, we felt enormous pride – I did, especially, as captain – that the team had played so well. The cheers of the crowd left a warm glow inside us for a long time afterwards.

The Hungarian politicians felt a warm glow too.

Barcs: Football was outrightly political. In parliament, for example, the First Secretary was always making references to the Golden Squad. He pronounced it as the direct result of socialism.

A few days later, the players were each presented with the Order of Merit in the reception room of the Presidential Council in parliament, in recognition of Hungarian football's finest hour. Puskas was promoted to the rank to which the British media, with their constant references to the 'galloping major', had already elevated him. At Wembley, he had only been, in truth, a 'galloping' captain.

Puskas: It was no small thing to put six past England in London. It was a fantastic match and the best team won. They hadn't been beaten on home soil by any continental team in ninety years of playing the game. Those of us who played – both the English and the Hungarian players, even the match officials – became firm friends after the match, a friendship that has lasted until today. I've always had a soft spot for Billy Wright. I know the Wembley game must have been a painful experience for English players and fans alike, but I must say they were one of the fairest groups of people I've ever met. I'll never forget the way everyone we encountered in England hailed the victory without resentment.

6

The World Cup, 1954

'In the end, we lost because we forgot that a match lasts for ninety minutes.'

Under the leadership of Imre Nagy, the 'softer' Hungarian regime attempted to proceed with its New Course. Several communist and social democrat political prisoners were released from the camps and prisons, but considerable resistance to the changes were maintained by the old Stalinists, led principally by the ousted Rakosi, who remained in key positions within the Party and the state bureaucracy. Deep resentment at the growing failure of the government to break free from its old, repressive ways, despite Stalin's death, sparked off the first stirrings of revolt amongst some journalists and writers in Budapest.

Meanwhile the Golden Squad continued on its majestic course, already world champions in all but name and on target for a World Cup Final in Switzerland in June 1954. News of England's defeat at Wembley had reverberated around the globe and, even outside Hungary, most experts expected Puskas and his team to beat anyone, including Brazil and the world champions Uruguay. Inside Hungary, expectations were reaching fever pitch.

Puskas: We could feel the build-up to the World Cup begin as early as spring 1953. For a start, everybody was talking about it non-stop. Unbeaten for three years, we were clear favourites and the whole population was desperate for us to win; it was almost palpable. There was little debate about the team. Everyone knew the best squad: fifteen players of whom almost any eleven would do, with four very good reserves. I didn't have any particular worries during the approach to the event. I knew my capabilities and wasn't afraid. I knew it was coming and that, as far as the country was concerned, we had to win it. But it is, after all, only sport. I never felt justified in worrying myself to death over it. We played well right up to the World Cup competition in Switzerland, and through it too. The only thing that went wrong was the final.

Sebes: 'We started serious preparations for the World Cup in December 1953. I took the squad, along with wives and children, to the Honved rest-house on Lake Balaton, and for the first three weeks the players trained on exercises four times a day. In the new year, with the players now back at home, we began more intensive physical preparations: cross-country running in the mornings, work in the indoor fitness centre in the afternoons. The lads also continued training at their clubs, of course, but every other afternoon the national team would play a match, even on frozen pitches. Not everyone was too keen on so much physical work, but I managed to persuade them that it was necessary.

'In February 1954, we went to Egypt to take advantage of the mild conditions there and we played a few matches against local clubs. Then in April we had a big match – Hungary's 300th international – against the same 'old enemy' we had faced in the first match in 1902: Austria. We scraped a 1–0 win but didn't play well.'

Puskas and the politicians (1950–54)

For four years, Puskas had led a charmed life at the heart of one of the most repressive regimes in Eastern Europe. Virtually alone in a country where even the most senior politicians and Party bosses were vulnerable to unpredictable changes of fortune, sudden arrest, torture and execution, Puskas seemed veritably untouchable.

The 'golden boy' at the head of the Golden Squad was paraded as an exemplar of the wisdom and justice of Hungarian socialism. Here was a poor lad from Kispest with a huge talent that symbolized the genius dormant in the working-class. Equipped and freed by the state to properly prepare and train, the football team he led took on the world's best and came away victorious. He was a jewel in the Hungarian communists' crown, and when there were medals to be doled out to workers who had produced more than their 'norm' – the so-called 'Stakhanovites' – who better than Puskas, a true footballing Stakhanovite himself, to present the prizes?

Though Puskas may have been the favourite of a hated and feared regime, ironically he was also respected and held in genuine affection by the mass of Hungarians who suffered under it. Though the fans of Ferencvaros always gave Puskas a hard time, some holding him responsible for the demise of their club through the luring away of their best players – like Kocsis and Czibor – to Honved, most people liked his rough-diamond style. He retained the 'common touch' and was often seen kicking a ball about with kids in the street. The stories of his smuggling exploits were legendary, and of course some envy and resentment did arise. But by and large, people admired his enterprise and his refusal to knuckle under and lead a quiet life. Perhaps most of all, Hungarians recognized something of themselves in him: a certain wayward genius, spontaneity and a fundamental enjoyment of life.

They also admired his off-hand treatment of the great and the powerful. In the company of some of the most feared political bosses in the country, Puskas could get away with behaviour that would have cost any other man his liberty, even his life.

Sebes: 'Puskas was a bit of a rough diamond with a rather direct manner that unnerved some people. Sometimes he let his mouth run away with him, even scolding politicians who weren't used to it at all. But he certainly had courage and beneath the rough exterior was a heart of gold.'

Szepesi: I remember after the 3–0 defeat of the Italians in Rome, in 1953, there was a dinner organized in Budapest to celebrate Puskas's 50th cap. The Minister of Defence, Mihaly Farkas, played host and at the high point of the evening presented Puskas with a set of silver cutlery for twenty-four people. When Puskas stood up to reply, he pulled out a decorated silver vase and presented it to Farkas on behalf of the team for the help they had received from the state. Farkas was surprised and a little taken aback by this, and protested that he couldn't possibly accept such a gift. But Puskas interrupted his protests, shouting, 'Keep it, old fellow, you never know what the future brings!' When you think how vulnerable those 'old guard' politicians were after Stalin's death, it was a funny remark, but also one very close to the bone.

Tichy: Mihaly Farkas really did like Puskas a lot and consequently he got away with things others only dreamed of. Once the team was staying in the Generals' Rest House – a magnificent facility on Margaret Island – and Farkas suddenly turned up, dressed head to foot in a completely white, general's uniform. Puskas just laughed out loud when he saw him: 'I thought you were the ice-cream boy, at last!' he shouted at Farkas. The place went quiet. I mean, this man had the power of life and death in Hungary in those days.

Vandor: They used to hold regular banquets at Honved after a big victory. At one of these dinner parties, I remember, a new Defence Minister was there called Nogradi. Puskas was vigorously complaining to him about some problems the players were facing that he wanted Nogradi to sort out. The politician was getting a bit cheesed off with it all and said, 'All right, all right, don't worry. I'll get something done about it, okay.' But that wasn't good enough for Puskas. He turned angrily on the Defence Minister: 'No, it's not okay. Go and do something about it NOW!' That's how he spoke to them sometimes. He wasn't even slightly interested in politics – only football counted.

It was stories like these, circulating around Hungary, which marked Puskas out in the public's mind as a 'one-off', an outlandish and gifted individual whom even the might of a fearsome police state could not entirely repress.

Tichy: Puskas more or less ran the Honved club, at least the footballing side of it. There was no strict training time for him, he was often there before us and stayed on after we'd gone. He worked on his own game, ball skills mostly. If he didn't feel like training – which was rare – he would say to the chief coach Jeno Kalmar, 'You do my training for me today!' Before a match, the doctor usually decided the lunch menu, say roast meat and mashed potatoes, but if Puskas wanted stew, that's what we got.

He had a freedom few others had. I remember once we were travelling from the Kispest ground to the pastry shop on the first floor of the splendid Beke Hotel. There were nine of us in Kocsis's old Mercedes which was a real banger of a car. If you wanted to indicate right, Budai had to thrust his hand out of the nearside window. A policeman was watching as we all spilled out of the car at the hotel. Puskas was last out, so he shouts back into the empty car, so loud the police can hear: 'The rest of you better stay in there, lads, there's police out here!' Even abroad, the parties continued. After a match, Puskas, Bozsik and Lorant would head off for the bars, taking me with them to make sure they got back safely when they'd had enough. If Puskas hadn't been recognized within two minutes of our entering a bar, we moved on to the next one.

Leading a team unbeaten in over three years towards an apparently inevitable World Cup victory, Puskas was, for a while at least, perhaps the only free man in Hungary.

World Cup preparations: Hungary 7 England 1

As part of both Hungary's and England's preparations for the World Cup, the national teams met one another in Budapest in May 1954, at the magnificent Nepstadion which was still under construction. Syd Owen came in at centre-half for England; Tom Finney played left-wing, with Ivor Broadis at inside-left. Poor Gil Merrick was still in goal.

Puskas: Our last match before leaving for Switzerland was against England in Budapest. It was the return leg of the 6–3 Wembley game and, for us, it was a beautiful performance. We all played very well and ran out 7–1 winners.

Owen: They probably made the England players too comfortable in their dressing-rooms. At the Nep Stadium, the changing-rooms were the most luxurious that I've ever changed in. There were easy-chairs all around, individual cupboards for players' clothes; but sitting in a nice easy-chair isn't the best preparation for playing an international match.

Merrick: 'The dressing-rooms are like a palace. The main changing-room is thirty yards long and about fifteen yards in width. The walls are oak-panelled and there are carpets laid down the centre of the floor. Down the middle, too, are armchairs and settees, and tables with beautiful vases of flowers on them. In fact, when we first walked in, we had to make sure we were not in the directors' room.' (Merrick, 1954, p.96)

Puskas: Everyone wanted a ticket for that match. A million people applied* but officially only 100,000 could get into the Nepstadion, though many more got in on the day of the match. Some even took pigeons in with them to send their tickets back

* One in nine of the Hungarian population.

out to friends. And the entire country listened to the game on the radio. The English were coming from a 1–0 defeat in Yugoslavia and stayed at Lake Balaton before the game with us. The weather was boiling hot that week, and you could see it hurt them more than it hurt us. We got an early goal again – a Lantos free-kick in the eighth minute – and they didn't look at all happy afterwards. Within minutes we realized that the English hadn't even changed their tactics since our last encounter, which was a big surprise. They just played the same; it was the only way they knew how to play and they stuck to it. Naturally, we knew what to do to take them apart. England weren't a bad team, but what with the heat and going three goals down quite soon, their heads began to drop. Finney was probably their best player, but in the end he only got away from his marker, Buzanszky, once or twice. We were fitter and faster than the English – in better all-round condition. The Hungarian fans loved it.

Sebes: 'We had to prove the 6–3 wasn't an accident. Although the English hadn't allowed us to train on the pitch at Wembley, we let them practise at the Nepstadion. We played even better than we had in London; I'd slightly adjusted the tactics and the English were lost. We were also too quick for them. Walter Winterbottom was very depressed after the game.'

Merrick: 'They have no centre-forward, as we know it, but rather three inside-forwards. The English idea of an inside-forward is a player who toils up and down the middle of the field, fetching and carrying. But how different the Hungarian inside-men play. They are attackers and nothing else. Their wingers hold touchline positions while their own defence is busy, but once the ball comes forward into attack, the wingers begin switching and quite likely one of them will come racing through the middle as a centre-forward. The wingers, like the rest of the team, do not hold the ball and dribble with it. In complete contrast to the English, the Hungarian wingers hardly ever cross a ball; in fact, only one centre was made in the whole of the game.' (Merrick, 1954, p.93-4)

Owen: My way of trying to cope with Hidegkuti was to try and read each individual situation and then decide whether to go with him or stay where I was. But they were so superior we just couldn't contain them. They had so much quality, not only in attack but from the depth of defence. They'd all got great individual skill and talent. (K&S)

Finney: 'Six or seven of them deserve to rank amongst the greatest the world has ever seen, yet their brilliance was always submerged for the general good of the team. I felt sorry for Syd Owen, gallantly trying to tackle the onslaught from the fantastic Puskas, Kocsis and Hidegkuti. What a terrifying experience for Syd in his second international.' (Finney, 1960, p.78)

Merrick: 'Never before in the whole of my career in professional football had I picked the ball out of the net seven times. It was impossible to think of anything else but goals in Budapest. When the Hungarians scored three times in four minutes to make it 6–0 mid-way through the second half, I frankly wondered just how gigantic the catastrophe enveloping us would be. Our defence, beaten by the speed of the Hungarian forwards allied to brilliantly accurate passing, was helpless to do anything about it.' (Merrick, 1954, p.91)

Finney: 'Ivor Broadis is a great comedian. I remember when he had taken off his boots after the Budapest match, he warned everyone, "Don't touch them unless you're wearing gloves, they're red hot." He added: "It's the first time I've ever come off the pitch with a sunburned tongue!" ' (Finney, 1960, p.78-9)

A young Johnny Haynes was among the reserves for England.

Haynes: I was only on the bench, thank God. I wouldn't have liked to have been out on the pitch that day, because they really hammered us. The pace they showed was something we weren't used to, pace with and without the ball. Everyone in the team was quick. They'd been playing together for three years or more, and they knew exactly what everybody was going to do. An unbelievably great side. (K&S)

Finney: 'England were bewitched, yes, and bothered and bewildered, by a side of soccer sorcerers who, at times, seemed capable of reading each other's minds. This was the nearest thing to telepathy on a football field, and I doubt if it's like will ever be reproduced again in my lifetime.' (Finney, 1960, p.78.)

Malcolm Allison, then a West Ham player, spoke to Syd Owen in England a week later.

Allison: We played Luton the Saturday after England lost 7–1 and I went up and shook hands with Syd before the game. I said, 'How was it over there, Syd, playing against the Hungarians?' He said, 'Malcolm, it was like playing people from outer space.' (K&S)

World Cup preliminaries

Puskas: We had put a number of good games together during the build-up. There were no real worries and I knew we could turn it on when the chips were down. Some observers thought they saw a certain apprehension in the team as the World Cup approached. Perhaps there was a little nervousness. So much was expected of us.

Sebes: 'During the competition, we all stayed at the Krone hotel in Solothurn, not far from Berne. Marton Bukovi was assisting me, with special responsibility for watching opponents training and in match-play. Just before the World Cup began, there was a congress of European FA representatives, and it was there that UEFA was established and the European Champions' Cup inaugurated.'

Puskas: Our first match in Switzerland was a warm-up against Luxembourg, whom we beat 10–0. The opening game for us in the World Cup was against South Korea – whom we beat 9–0. We knew absolutely nothing about them, of course. They were complete beginners in the world game at the time – they're much better now – and they didn't have a chance really.

Despite the end of the Korean war a year earlier, there were no commercial flights out of Korea in 1954. The footballers underwent a six-day ordeal by road, rail, sea and air to make it to Switzerland. Half the squad were routed via Tokyo and had flown to Europe in a US military aircraft; the diminutive Koreans sitting in huge seats designed for American airborne troops, their legs dangling like children's. With less than a day's rest, they faced the Hungarians, and half the Korean team was down with cramp within twenty minutes.

Puskas: The next game was against West Germany and we beat them easily, 8–3. If you add the game against England in Budapest, we had scored thirty-four goals in the last four matches. I got injured during the match against Germany and missed the next two games, against Brazil and Uruguay, both of which we won 4–2. It wasn't that the German match was especially tough – in fact it was more like a friendly, they showed such little resistance – but Leibrich *[the German defender]* caught me from behind, my leg went and I had to be taken off. I think we were 6–1 up at the time and we finished with ten men. I was not happy. I remember in the dressing-room after coming off, the team doctor *[Laszlo Kreisz]* was prodding my leg here and there, and I said, 'Pour cold water on it, it won't get better with you just prodding it.'

Sebes: 'There were 50,000 German fans there to support their team, but the referee should never have allowed those fouls by Leibrich on Puskas. The first was in the penalty area and he didn't give it, but the third foul was vicious and left our captain with a badly swollen ankle and out of the competition.'

Hungary's easy defeat of West Germany, who were not at all fancied to win the competition, caused no surprise to anyone. But Sepp Herberger, the coach of the unseeded German squad, had other ideas, as his assistant – and later successor – Helmut Schoen recalled:

Schoen: 'Nobody but Hungary was expected to win in 1954. That was the opinion in Germany, too. Hungary were undoubtedly the best team. But when Germany played them in the first round, Sepp Herberger knew he could qualify for the quarter-finals even while losing to Hungary, so he deliberately did not field his strongest side against the Hungarians. It was a shrewd move because it meant that, whereas he knew the exact formation and strengths of the Hungarians, the formation of the German team in the final would be new to Sebes.' (Miller, 1981, p.39)

The 'Battle of Berne'

For the quarter-final match against Brazil, with Puskas injured, Sebes moved Czibor to inside-left and played the two Toths (Jozsef and Mihaly) on either wing. Three players, including two Brazilians, were sent off in a violent match refereed by the Englishman Arthur Ellis, and watched by the journalist and writer, Brian Glanville.

Glanville: 'The quarter-finals pitted Hungary against Brazil at Berne, in a match which was destined to become notorious. The 'Battle of Berne', as it has become known, has in retrospect been blamed chiefly on Brazil. Theirs were the first and greater excesses on the field, theirs the shameful, brutal invasion of the Hungarian dressing-room after the game.' (Glanville, 1973, p.93)

Ellis: 'I am convinced, after all these years of reflection, that the infamous "Battle of Berne" was a battle of politics and religion. The politics of the Communist Hungarians and the religion of the Catholic Brazilians. My own blood was boiling later on. Not because a Brazilian woman spat on my car window as I left the Berne stadium, and not because I was greeted with shouts of *Communista*. The FIFA disciplinary committee sadly let down the principle of refereeing by failing to deal with the two Brazilians and one Hungarian sent off summarily, and passing on the files of their cases to their own respective football associations.' (Ellis, 1962, p.156–7)

The Hungarians went ahead within three minutes with a Hidegkuti goal, and Kocsis got the second shortly afterwards. But Djalma Santos scored from the penalty spot to keep Brazil in the match.

Puskas: I had to watch the game from the stands, but the team played brilliantly against Brazil. We went two-up within ten minutes and the Brazilians lost their heads a bit. It became a very hard and skilful match.

The second half saw the worst behaviour. A Lantos penalty put the Hungarians ahead 3–1, but again the Brazilians came back following a wonderful extended dribble and shot from Julinho. Bozsik retaliated after a tackle from Nilton Santos and both players were sent off. Kocsis made it 4–2 for Hungary in the final minute, though there was still time for the Brazilian inside-left Humberto Tozzi to get expelled from the pitch for kicking Lorant. The dying minutes of the game were little more than a running fight.

Sebes: 'This was a battle; a brutal, savage match. The Brazilian winger Maurinho stepped on Jozsef Toth's leg and tore the muscle. We strapped him up but in reality he was one of the walking wounded. Santos kicked and punched Bozsik and the ref sent both of them off. At the end we had won 4–2, but it wasn't over yet. Brazilian photographers and fans flooded on to the pitch and police were called to clear it. Maurinho and Buzanszky clashed in the tunnel and a small war broke out in the corridor to the dressing-rooms. Everyone was having a go; fans, players and officials. I got a bottle in the face and needed four stitches afterwards.'

World Cup referee Mervyn Griffiths witnessed some of the events from the stands.

Griffiths: 'Immediately the final whistle was blown pandemonium broke loose. Brazilian reserves and trainers ran on to the field and the few police seemed powerless to check the fights that started. I saw one policeman have his legs kicked from under him yet he did nothing. The trouble began in the tunnel leading to the dressing-rooms. Broken bottles and football boots were used as weapons.' (Griffiths, 1958, p.76)

There were rumours that Puskas had attacked the Brazilian centre-half Pinheiro, striking him in the face with a bottle.

Puskas: The big problem came after the match. Two players started fighting in the tunnel and the Brazilian came off worse. Next thing, the whole Brazilian team was up in arms and there were fierce arguments going on. Light bulbs were smashed; Sebes got hit by a bottle – or was it a soda syphon? – which cut his eyebrow, and I grabbed one of the Brazilians and dragged him into our dressing-room. He was terrified and I ended up letting him go. I don't suppose the whole incident took more than three or four minutes, but it was quite nasty.

The semi-final

Puskas: In the semi-final against Uruguay, both Hidegkuti and Palotas played. Our team was a little battered and bruised with only three days' rest after the Brazil game, and the match went to extra time. We won though, 4–2.

This proved a much more civilized affair than the previous game, and the standard of football certainly impressed Welshman Griffiths, who refereed the match with the hopefully named Scotsman, Charlie Faultless, as one of his linesmen. For the Hungarians, Budai replaced the injured Toth and Palotas came in for Mihaly Toth. Kocsis was the star of the match, scoring two headed goals in extra time. *

Griffiths: 'Reporters described it as the greatest game of football ever seen and who am I to contradict them? Straight from the kick-off we saw some magnificent play by both sides, while an early foul by a Hungarian player gave me the chance to show I was going to stand no nonsense. From that point on, there were no incidents to which anyone could take exception. The match had everything – brilliant individual runs, excellent combined moves and marvellous saves by both goalkeepers.

'With the closing minutes approaching and Hungary leading 2–1, we had a scene rarely witnessed on a football field. A Uruguayan *[Hohberg]* scored the equalizing goal and, though there was no other player near, immediately fell to the ground. Evidently the excitement of scoring the vital goal was too much for him and he had fainted. He was still being attended to when I blew the final whistle, but he was able to take his place with the rest of the team when they took the field for extra time.' (Griffiths, 1958, p.77)

Sebes: 'After ninety minutes, the team's morale was terribly

* Kocsis was voted Best Player of the 1954 World Cup.

low. We'd been 2–0 up until the last fifteen minutes and couldn't believe it had gone to extra time. I tried my best to raise their spirits. I told Palotas to play further forward and criss-cross the pitch while Hidegkuti moved back and forward. Schiaffino was Uruguay's best player and he nearly put them ahead straight after the restart. My assistant Mandi, next to me on the bench, went pale. We probably wouldn't have made it back if we'd gone behind then.

'Then came our moment: into the second period, Budai crossed and Kocsis nodded it in. Five minutes later, Bozsik bounced another in off Kocsis's head and it was all over. It was a very different affair from the Brazilian game. The Uruguayan captain came to the dressing-room afterwards to shake our hands in congratulation. It took us all by surprise; these men were real sportsmen.'

Puskas: From my seat in the stand, I was really proud of the team's performance that day. They showed fantastic heart against a very good Uruguayan side.

The final: Hungary 2 West Germany 3

Puskas had not played since the first German match.

Glanville: 'The great question before the final was whether Puskas would play. He would, said the reports. He wouldn't. He was hoping to. There was no chance. There was a fifty-fifty chance; a specialist had said so. The ankle was better. It would never recover in time. Electrical treatment had failed, the Germans' underwater massage had been spurned. In the event, however, Puskas *did* play.' (Glanville, 1973, p.100)

Puskas: I was desperate to get fit for the final. I got lots of letters and telegrams from friends and fans at home, wishing me well. I'd had to sit there watching the team with my fingers crossed and I was really glad that they continued to play so well. My leg was examined twice a day but it wasn't until three or four days before the final that I could really move it properly and I could do some training. It was only the day before the match that I was passed fit by the medics and Sebes gave me a fitness test. But everyone could see that my leg was OK. I certainly wasn't the weakest player in our team in that match, which turned out to be a very unlucky one for us. It was against the Germans again, of course, whom we had beaten so easily in the preliminary round. In the end, we lost because we forgot that a match lasts for ninety minutes.

Sebes: 'Just before the final, the doctor, myself and the other coaches all agreed that Puskas should play. Since his withdrawal, Kocsis had had two men marking him every game and I knew Puskas would draw off some of that attention. I was always happy to have Puskas, Kocsis and Hidegkuti down the middle, but I wasn't sure about the flanks. My right-winger, Budai, looked exhausted to me after the semi, and Jozsef Toth was still injured. In the end I decided to play Czibor on the right and Mihaly Toth on the left. Czibor had never played there in the national team, but he used to play wide on the right for Komarom. I wanted him to keep Kohlmeyer busy in the German defence, making more room for Puskas and Kocsis to do their worst. I told Hidegkuti to stay deep and, along with Toth, to give defensive cover. Everyone was glad to have Puskas back, of course.

'But the night before the match was dreadful. It was the evening of the Swiss national brass-band competition, with parades until two in the morning, right outside our hotel. They started playing again just after lunch on the day of the final, when the players want an hour's sleep if they can get it.

'And then the rain. It rained all day before the final, and very heavily during the second half as well. The ground was soft, very muddy and tiring for players. At first we couldn't even get into the stadium. By the time we arrived the place was full and sealed off by police. The German bus had passed through a few minutes before us, but we were not allowed through and had to park up outside and walk through the heaving crowd to get in. I was furious, and that was before I got hit with the butt of a policeman's rifle as I tried to explain that we were the Hungarian team to play in the final.'

Puskas: We played Czibor on the right wing that day because the German left-back, Kohlmeyer, was thought quite slow. It wasn't long before we were two goals up in the first half. I got the first and Czibor the second. We had at least half a dozen other clear chances to score which were missed. Then we sat back and tried to keep the ball in midfield to neutralize the game and tire the Germans out. We played with Hidegkuti lying deep as usual, and though the Germans (like the English) played a very traditional 'WM' formation, our tactic did not have the same devastating effect that it had at Wembley. The Germans had filmed the 6–3 match and had obviously studied it for some time, because they seemed to know exactly what to expect. Mind you, after the run of success we'd had – 36 internationals, with 32 victories and 4 draws at the time – the world's press had been full of us and everyone knew us and wanted to beat us.

Sebes: 'There were only five surviving players from the German side we had beaten 8–3 a couple of weeks before. We started well and scored two quite quickly, but the team seemed to get increasingly nervous after Zakarias's back-pass had allowed them to get one back. At half-time, everyone was complaining about the ref.'*

* Bill Ling of England had also refereed the first match against Germany.

Thirty thousand West Germans had crossed the Swiss border to support their team, but most Hungarians were not allowed to travel abroad.

Puskas: Of course, there weren't very many Hungarian fans in the crowd, it was mostly German or neutral but when we heard the German fans chant, 'Come on, Germany', we heard our own supporters reply in kind. At that level, it is necessary when you go ahead early to take some of the steam out of the game and ration your energy. We had had a tough series of games up to the Final, especially against Brazil and Uruguay. The Germans had had a much easier progress. After the downpour – which never did our football much good – the pitch got very heavy, mud everywhere. We gave two silly goals away, the first when Zakarias attempted to pass the ball back to our goalie Groscis, and it got stuck in the surface water. The second came from a cross on the left. Grosics and Lorant were arguing about who should clear the ball, they both missed it and Rahn scored from five metres out.

In the second half, the Hungarians did everything they could to regain the lead. Hidegkuti hit the post, Kocsis the bar, Kohlmeyer blocked on the line and the German keeper Turek pulled off an inspired and spectacular series of saves. With only six minutes to go, Rahn scored his second goal, a powerful shot that picked up speed off the watery surface. The Hungarians attacked with even greater frenzy and with two minutes left, they thought they had levelled the score.

Puskas: I got an equalizer right at the death but that Welsh linesman Griffiths, who had refereed the Uruguay match, disallowed it for offside, even though the English ref, Bill Ling, had given it. We were already back at the centre-circle by the time he flagged. I'll never forgive him for that. We didn't argue – not on the pitch anyway – and the Germans won. We hung our heads. What could we do? We couldn't beat up the linesman, that's for sure, but I was pretty mad.

Griffiths: 'With the minutes ticking away, Hungary fought desperately for the equalizer and actually got the ball in the net, but as I had previously flagged for offside the score did not count. Puskas came over to me and gave me a dirty look.' (Griffiths, 1958, p.79)

Puskas: In the end, we deserved what we got. We should never have relaxed after going two up; we should have pressed on then, looking for the third to kill the game off. The defeat wasn't the result of any element of our training or preparation. It was our own fault: we thought we had the match won, gave two stupid goals away and let them back into it.

My fitness hadn't wavered, even in the mud; I'd scored one, and that disallowed goal right at the end as well. I couldn't believe the offside decision and nor could millions of others when they saw it. I mean, it was almost a minute afterwards when he raised the flag; we thought we were back in it. I could have murdered him, it was one of the very worst moments in my whole career and we were well and truly sick about it. To lose the World Cup on such a decision, it wasn't right. Some of our players wondered if there was something more sinister about it, but eventually I forgave the linesman and shook his hand when we met in England years later.

Sebes: 'During the ninety minutes, the Germans had eight shots and scored three goals; we had twenty-five shots and scored twice, with one disallowed. And isn't it odd that we always seemed to get British referees?'

Grosics: I felt – and still feel – an enormous, personal sense of loss; that something went out of my life that has never been restored in the decades that followed. Even today, when I am asked to talk about those years with the Golden Squad, it's always there in the back of my mind. And there's absolutely nothing we can do about it. We cannot replay the game to prove we were the better side. On the day, they beat us, and in doing so perhaps revealed a deep self-conceit in the team that had never showed itself before. After we got the second goal in the eighth minute, we thought it was all over.

That match was lost by us not won by the Germans. It was the saddest day in the history of Hungarian football. It shattered the myth – our legendary status – and neither the experts nor the general public at home could bear it. It's more than forty years ago now, but if someone was to wake me up tomorrow morning and remind me of that match, I'd burst into tears. (K&S)

7

The Aftermath

'If there is no friendship, there is no football.'

The World Cup Final defeat sparked a mini-uprising in Budapest, a small dress rehearsal for what was to come fifteen months later. No one expected the impact of the Hungarian team's failure to be so profound, but then hardly anyone had seriously considered the likelihood that they might get beaten at all, certainly not by West Germany.

Sebes: 'On the way home we were very nervous, but we did our best to disguise it and everyone was very disciplined and sportsmanlike. If we had been beaten by a better team I wouldn't have minded second place, and I honestly had no idea that it would affect Hungarians in the same hot-headed way that defeat had affected the Brazilians. If someone had told me in Switzerland what I could expect at home, I would never have believed them. I was blamed for making too many excuses and a bad team selection. My memories of returning home are so sad and painful. The whole world expected us to win and it was a huge burden on the players.'

Barcs: I was out of favour at the time, not allowed to attend the World Cup. I sat at home listening to Szepesi on the radio. When we lost, there were grown men weeping in the streets. I was one of them myself.

Sebes: 'We knew nothing about what had been happening in Budapest. We saw only that 30,000 fans awaited the returning Austrian team – our great rivals – after they had achieved *third* place; there was a huge crowd to greet them at the station in Vienna. I didn't expect an official delegation to meet us at the border, but one did, and we were told not to return to Budapest but to go to the training camp at Tata for a dinner with government officials. I knew the players were dying to get home to their families.'

Barcs: I was sent to Vienna to meet them on their way home – I wasn't good enough to go to Switzerland but good enough to be a 'victim'. Some people were afraid even then that some of the players might defect.

Szepesi: At the Hungarian border we were met by Zoltan Vas *[a senior politician]*. We were all taken to the Tata training camp, players, coaches and journalists like me. At the camp, Rakosi and Farkas awaited us. There was a gloomy dinner with a short speech from Rakosi. Everyone was absolutely down.

Sebes: 'The Minister of the Interior sat next to me at the table. At one point he said, "Are you nervous? Don't worry, we will defend your family and your flat from attack." I felt sick in the pit of my stomach as he told me that there had been demonstrations all over the country, but especially in the capital, which had turned into anti-government riots, with thousands outside the offices of *Nepsport* and in front of the Party press office.'

Vandor: Hungary has never been so disappointed in its entire history. It wasn't just football fans, the whole country seemed to collapse under the weight of the loss. If they'd won, Puskas could have been Prime Minister if he'd wanted. Instead, he was partially blamed. Crowds were overturning trams in the centre of Budapest by evening time.

Szepesi: My flat was guarded for a few days afterwards. The players were accused by some of taking money to lose the match.

Puskas: The team didn't deserve what happened in Hungary immediately afterwards. The place was like a funeral. There had been great crowds to send us off to Switzerland, but very few came to receive us home. The average Hungarian fan didn't know a great deal about world football. They thought we were *bound* to win the World Cup, although Sebes had always tried to emphasize that winning wasn't guaranteed. The Hungarian media hadn't helped matters, but after four years without defeat it was only natural that everyone expected it to go on and on.

Supporters joined the chorus of disappointment after the Final and I did my best to close my ears to it all, otherwise I would have gone insane. There were lots of rumours and paranoid fantasies: that we'd sold the game for a Mercedes car each and such nonsense. (There are people who still believe that today.) How could you imagine a football team selling a World Cup Final? Young lads and drunks tried to provoke us in public. When it's good they sing; when it's bad they swear; we'd heard it all before but never this vitriolic.

Sebes: 'In the weeks that followed, I was publicly insulted and received hate mail. At first I tried to explain by letter to people, but it was useless. At least the press were more reasonable.'

Puskas: The police and military asked us not to go out for a few days till things calmed down, so we stayed out of sight. It was a little like we were in mourning too, coming to terms with the defeat. To be frank, it was all a bit of a mess for a while, but things soon got back on course. In Hungary, everything only lasts a while until people let off steam.

My injury – and the decision to play me in the final – came in for great attention, of course. Some said I should never have played; that I demanded a place only to make sure that I personally lifted that cup. It wasn't true. I would never have been selected if I hadn't been able to demonstrate my fitness to the coaches and the doctor. But what can you say? There's no point arguing with people who are already convinced they know everything. The really strange thing is not that we lost one match, but that we had been able to win so many. The fact is that on that day, the team was carrying a couple of other injuries too, and everyone was tired. When the torrent of rain fell, it changed the conditions radically and it's always a case of who likes the heavy going better. The Germans seemed to get stronger in the wet conditions; they kept going. We should never have let them off the hook after going two goals up, and once they were ahead it was hard to get back into it.

Szepesi: I think Sebes had to play Puskas in the final and it wasn't the player's fault that we lost. I think there may have been a problem in that the coach, the doctor and all the trainers were totally preoccupied with Puskas's fitness and whether he should play. They perhaps forgot about the fitness of others. I arrived at the training camp on the Wednesday night; there was no training Thursday, and only light training on Friday. Saturday was taken up with watching Puskas try out his leg. I think it was a mistake to move Czibor to the right; Budai should have played there.

Barcs: People said it was Puskas, not Sebes, who picked the side. The MTK winger Sandor should have played, instead of Czibor on the right.

Vandor: Some people thought Puskas had only been concerned with picking that cup up himself. Few said it in public, but it was in the air. The truth is that he scored a goal, had another disallowed and was by no means the worst Hungarian player on the day. But there were all kinds of wild rumours running around: that they'd been drinking and womanizing before the match, things like that. And people thought of Puskas as being as much in charge of the team as Sebes.

Following the World Cup, Puskas came in for some serious barracking at Honved's away matches and at one point he quit the field – just walked off – in protest (an incident not reported in the Hungarian press). Predictably he got the worst abuse from Ferencvaros fans, and Kalman Vandor remembers Puskas dropping his shorts on one occasion in response to the catcalls. Honved dropped him for a few matches to avoid trouble and so did Sebes, though the coach insisted that Puskas was still playing brilliantly but was in danger of losing confidence in the face of such barracking. Grosics, with his background as a politically 'unreliable' person, found himself in much deeper trouble.

Grosics arrested

Grosics: A few months after the World Cup, in November 1954, I was arrested for the second time, on suspicion of spying and treason. It was just minutes before the kick-off of a league match – I was warming up on the pitch – when I received an order to return to the dressing-room, where I was told, without explanation, that I could no longer play football in Hungary.

I still don't know who denounced me to the authorities. It was another two months before I even knew the charges against me. I was 'under examination' for fifteen months, twice getting pulled in to 'Fo utca', the street with the AVH's interrogation centre and prison. There were many other 'suspects' in there and you never knew whether someone was going to finger you just to save themselves.

It was a terrible, terrifying experience. No one who has not lived through such times can understand what it was like. In those days there were 'show trials', forced confessions, summary executions. If they pleased, the AVH could just simply beat you to death; no one would know. The fear under interrogation – even if you were not being physically abused – was horrifying.

Needless to say, I was not allowed to play football during this period. In fact, I couldn't even enter a football ground. But at the end of fifteen months I was officially discharged from suspicion with the hardly glowing phrase, 'Lack of evidence'. I had missed twenty-three international matches by the time I was selected again. A month after my discharge, on the orders of the political bosses, I was told – without any consultation – that I was to join the miners' club Tatabanya, and there I stayed for seven years. It meant exile for me, though in time I enjoyed the people there and was glad of the simple, human warmth they offered after what I'd been through. My family had to remain in Budapest, so I constantly travelled back and forth to see them.

Vandor: After Puskas, Grosics had the biggest mouth. He said too much for those times. He was openly critical of the regime and that meant trouble. That's why he was 'banished' to Tatabanya.

This time, neither Puskas nor Sebes was able to influence the authorities. The two men's stars were waning and their political connections wearing thin. Grosics was on his own.

Grosics: During the time of my arrest, even my best friends avoided me. I couldn't easily contact anyone. My house was watched, so no one dared approach. For fifteen months it was like house-arrest. I certainly couldn't leave Budapest. I couldn't turn to anyone. I think some of the players tried to intercede for me but the AVH warned them off, telling them, 'It's none of your business.' I still think I was 'shopped' by one of the other players, probably as someone who consorted too readily with foreigners during trips abroad. Those were terrible times; very hard to live through.

Afterwards for Puskas and Sebes

Puskas: Losing the World Cup Final – the first match we had lost in four years – was traumatic. Some of us were very low, but that team had great recuperative powers and, with one or two changes, we soon picked ourselves up and went into another good unbeaten run of eighteen consecutive games. That shut the moaners up, and soon we were playing as before, in front of 100,000 adoring fans in the Nepstadion. Aren't folks weird? But they don't like to admit it, do they?

The team's confidence and trust returned and life was calm for a while. We kept up the tactical experiments, constantly changing positions and remaining very fluid. Even small adjustments could cause major changes and new problems for the opposition. Playing Hidegkuti deep, for example, was our great tactical innovation (and the one which took the English completely by surprise), but it was just a case of dropping the No. 9 back a mere ten metres or so – simple, really. We kept experimenting with these tactical shapes in almost every game.

But things were never going to return to the way they had been. Today, Puskas tends to dismiss the memory of those dark days in 1954–55 as something which passed quickly and was soon forgotten. But when pressed, he admits the presence of a profoundly vengeful atmosphere in Budapest in the months that followed the World Cup defeat, much of it directed at Sebes.

Puskas: Everybody was looking for someone to blame. In the streets, people looked at me as if I had some kind of disease. Some people are idiots, aren't they? I think Sebes got the worst of it, though, because he was the most vulnerable. We were only players, but he was the manager. A lot of people put the boot in and we could see how much it hurt him. He aged a few years in as many weeks. For a while we had to be protected in public, with a couple of police officers minding us. If there is no friendship, there is no football.

Tichy: The loss of that final was nothing short of traumatic for Sebes. He was sometimes close to despair, and the mental wounding he got left scars. His son was badly beaten up at school, as well.

The matches against Scotland, and Honved v Wolves

In December 1954, the Hungarian national team played Scotland at Hampden Park. The Scots took the match very seriously, anxious to do better than the English had. Three full-scale practice matches were played by the Scotland team against league sides, in preparation for their encounter with the team everyone still considered to be the best in the world. As usual, the Hungarians got off to a good start, going two goals up in the first half-hour. At half-time, it was 3–1. In the second half, the Scots gave it everything and were later criticized for their 'hard tackling', especially for Lawrie Reilly's charge on the man replacing Grosics, the Hungarian keeper Farago. It knocked him out cold.

Puskas: We were surprised at how hard and tough the Scotland players were when we played them that year. They were not 'technical' players at all, but had real heart and gave it everything. They gave us two very hard games, but we beat them 4–2, and 3–1 back in Budapest later.

A few days after the Scotland match, Honved played Wolves, managed by Stan Cullis. Honved lost the 'friendly', 3–2. (Cullis had done his homework and flooded the pitch to make the ground very heavy.) Just as in the World Cup Final, the Hungarians went two-up early on, but ran into trouble as the second half wore on, finally succumbing to a hail of long balls in the mud, with the Wolves forward Swinbourne scoring twice.

Puskas: It was raining as usual in England when I went there with Honved. The pitch at Molineux was absolutely sodden and although we were two goals up, Wolves equalized in the second half and won with a doubtful penalty late in the game. Do you know who was refereeing that game? The same Welsh linesman who had denied us the equalizer in the World Cup Final. It was good to see Billy Wright again, though.

The return match against Scotland took place in May 1955. The Scots had a tough time getting into Hungary, with major delays at the border and soldiers accompanying them all the way to Budapest. Scotland's left-winger Billy Liddell was amazed at the fuss.

Liddell: 'Two soldiers accompanied us in the coach and stayed with us until the customs went through our things after arrival in Budapest, about nine o'clock in the evening. The hotel room in which this took place was decorated in red, and had busts and photographs all over the place of past and present Russian leaders. Before the match we were invited, along with the Hungarians, to a reception at the British Embassy, where we met and chatted – through interpreters, of course – with such famous figures as Ferenc Puskas, Nandor Hidegkuti, Joszef Bozsik, Sandor Kocsis and others. What struck me most forcibly about them at first was the sartorial elegance of all the Hungarian footballers, which stuck out all the more against the rather drably dressed ordinary folk of the city.' (Liddell, 1960, p.79)

Again the Scots performed with more credit than the English had a year earlier. Liddell missed a penalty in the second half and Scotland pressed hard to close the 3–1 scoreline. In the end, the Hungarian crowd cheered them from the field.

Political developments

The political situation in Hungary was deteriorating fast. In March 1955, the Central Committee denounced Imre Nagy's New Course policy, and within a few weeks the Prime Minister had been removed from all Party posts. Nagy was succeeded by Andras Hegedus, but it was Rakosi and his ultra-Stalinist supporters who were still running affairs.

In May the Warsaw Pact was established, with Hungary a founding member. Khrushchev and Bulganin visited Yugoslavia and admitted that Stalin's allegations against Tito had been trumped up. These admissions threatened Rakosi and other hard-liners in Hungary, because they themselves were implicated in the earlier prosecutions (and executions) of people like Laszlo Rajk and his companions. These had taken place in 1949, during the period of Stalin's complicated plotting against Tito after the war, but Rajk's widow was still alive in Hungary and seeking justice against those who had murdered her husband.

Any public criticism of Rakosi was rigorously suppressed. At the end of 1955, the former Prime Minister Nagy was expelled from the Party. Thus the process of 'de-Stalinization', which had probably advanced further in Hungary than in most other Eastern European states, ground to a halt.

Sebes: 'After the World Cup, I drew my own conclusions and continued to search for young talent to replace some of the older squad members.* It had to be planned properly. The Golden

* Fenyvesi replaced Czibor on the left; Zakarias gave way to Szojka or Kotasz; Varhidi came in for Lorant.

Team had not just appeared by chance. In 1955, I began consciously to prepare for the 1958 World Cup, but drafting in youngsters wasn't easy because this squad knew each other so well and sometimes resented newcomers.'

The Golden Squad began to put together another good run, scoring thirty goals in five matches during the month of May 1955. (Meanwhile, world champions West Germany played six, won two, lost four.) But good results were no longer sufficient to protect Sebes and others.

Sebes: 'Behind the scenes, attacks against me and one or two players continued. Just before we left for Switzerland in autumn 1955, it was decided in the Sports Ministry that the national coach shouldn't necessarily always travel with the team, and Sos Karoly was appointed for the Swiss game. He sat on the bench while I had to watch from the stands.

'Gradually, the successful "collective" that I had formed to run the national team was systematically broken up. Towards the end of the year, I attended a plenary session of UEFA and was elected chair of the committee to oversee the development of the European Championship for national teams. But when I returned to Budapest, I found that my secretary had been dismissed. The coaches that formed the nucleus of my 'think tank' were dispersed. Pal Titkos was sent to Egypt; Gyula Mandi went to Brazil; Gusztav Hidas to Nigeria.

'The old 'perks' were gradually withdrawn too. The players' smuggling began to cause more and more headaches. I found one player under arrest at a police station just three days before a match against Italy *[played 27 November 1955, Hungary won 2–0]*. Grosics was now unavailable and I lost another goalkeeper on smuggling charges. Czibor became increasingly unpredictable and started a pointless argument with Tichy on the way back from a tour in the Near East. I decided there and then that the brilliant winger, with such fantastic pace and touch, would never play for me again. I'd had enough of him.'

In January 1956 Honved toured Egypt and the following month Hungary were beaten by Turkey, 3–1 in Istanbul. Apart from the World Cup Final, this was their first loss since the spring of 1950. The most damaging defeat, however, came a few months later on a very wet day in May, when the Golden Squad suffered their first ever loss at the Nepstadion in Budapest, 4–2 against Czechoslovakia. They were never at their best in the rain. Puskas was under such constant barracking at home that Sebes didn't even select him for the match.

Sebes: 'I think the players were still tired from the earlier tour. I didn't dare play Puskas in the Nepstadion because there were so many attacks on him and his nerves were frayed at the edges. He would have been a liability. As it was, the team was draining confidence. Not long before, we had felt every match could be won.

'There was a huge difference now between the way we were treated at home and the welcome we got abroad. Attacks against us continued in Budapest. Some people said that 'personality cults' had developed on the football pitch; that the spotlight was for ever on Puskas, Bozsik and Kocsis; that they had taken up permanent residence in the national team and good youngsters were consequently ignored. But it wasn't true.

'The players were now facing very tough customs controls at the borders. Sometimes their houses were searched for no good reason. The politicians were keen to distract the public's attention from their own privileges. After all, the smuggling was virtually officially sanctioned; everyone knew about it. But it was only after the World Cup that we were attacked for it.'

Of all the players, Puskas bore the brunt of the blame. His influence on team selection – once judged so benign and gifted – was suddenly identified as overwhelming, and a sign of Sebes's weakness.

Sebes: 'Puskas never tried to tell me who to pick for the team; at most he would discuss the roles of some players. We never argued about team selection because he trusted me to look after the team's best interests. Even when I was strict with him, I knew he didn't mind. Some people told me our relationship was "too good".

'Puskas didn't waste words, and when he spoke it was usually worth listening to. He knew his place in the team was assured, and I think that had enabled him to relax much more than might otherwise have been the case. Of course he cared a great deal about who was around him in the team, but he didn't doubt my judgement.'

Puskas's weight problems

Despite Sebes's continuing loyalty, the truth was that Puskas's form was deteriorating – perhaps hardly surprising under the public onslaught he was facing – along with his level of fitness and mobility. He had increasingly faced difficulties keeping his weight down, but he was so skilful and inspired a player – capable of real pace, too, over short distances – and so often surrounded by other such gifted players that he could get away with carrying a belly some of the time. But as his age increased and his love of good food remained undiminished, and especially under the critical gaze of the post-1954 Hungarian public, it became increasingly obvious that he was over-indulging. The sports journalist Kalman Vandor remembers:

Vandor: When he was young, he didn't have a reputation for drinking and eating so much. It only emerged in the 1950s, largely after the great victories of the Golden Squad in the Olympic Games, and against England and Italy. I suppose he came to feel like the great star who could do what he liked. It wasn't drinking that was the problem. Perhaps sometimes he drank more than a sportsman should, but he was never drunk.

Food, however – well, he could eat masses of it. And of course, when he put on weight the fans and the media noticed immediately.

It is tempting to identify the origins of Puskas's heroic appetite in the hungry days of his childhood in the 1930s, when playing for a prize of Uncle Joszef's spicy sausages was one of the most memorable matches. When young Puskas joined the local football club, the promising youngsters at Kispest received 'extra rations' to help build them up. It may be that football and food became inextricably intertwined in Puskas's formative experiences: success at the former led to more of the latter. He certainly had a huge appetite for both.

Barcs: We had a lot of trouble trying to keep his weight down. He loved all those fatty Hungarian foods. In a good hotel, at meal-times in public he might only take the soup. But back in his room upstairs, Puskas would order the full menu: sausages, salami, bacon and *two* kilos of bread. He loved peanuts, too. I remember going to the cinema with him in Spain, and his pockets must have been full of them because he kept nibbling away all the time.

Geoffrey Green records a story told by Billy Wright about Puskas's prodigious eating habits in those days:

Green: 'Following the Wolves v Honved prestige match at Molineux in December 1954, Wright was struck by Puskas's enormous appetite at the banquet which concluded the night. It was as big as his capacity for work on the football field. Even at the end of a huge meal, when most of the guests had had enough, Puskas was still going strong. Wright watched, fascinated, as the Hungarian captain ate another dozen biscuits – precisely one dozen – laden with butter and Danish blue cheese. He caught Puskas's eye as biscuit after biscuit disappeared, pointing to his own waistline and shook his head in warning. Puskas just smiled –

and continued eating.' (Green, 1974, p.286-7)

Sebes sacked

In early July 1955, the Sports Ministry and the Hungarian FA held a joint meeting in Budapest. It produced a resolution stating that it had been a mistake to place the organization and control of the national team in only one person's hands, namely Sebes's. It said that the long years of success had lead to an unhealthy, over-sympathetic relationship between the coach and some of the players, with the consequence that the former had begun to indulge the latter. The football players, the statement continued, had become too privileged in comparison with other sportsmen.

Sebes: 'When we were abroad, my family back home sat in fear awaiting the results. My kids were terrified. What will happen to us if the team loses another match? Will they murder us? They begged me to resign, but I refused to listen to them.'

In March 1956, Hungary lost another match, away to Belgium 5–4, after leading 3–1 at half-time. The Golden Squad were showing an increasing vulnerability to surrendering a lead. Sebes was shortly to surrender his job.

Sebes: 'Finally, the FA and the Sports Ministry decided to put the affairs of the national team and the junior squads into the hands of a five-man committee. Bukovi took over as manager of the senior team, with Karoly Sos, Lajos Baroti, Karoly Lakat and Jeno Vincze helping to select the side and run the juniors. They were all put on a monthly salary – something I had never had, though I was paid for my work at the Sports Ministry.'

Sebes, however, for a while remained chairman of the Olympic Committee and he nominated a team full of young players for the coming Games in Melbourne, in the winter of 1956. He was soon informed by the committee that the team wouldn't be allowed to go because it hadn't prepared properly. Bukovi restored Czibor to the first team and Grosics was allowed to return, but otherwise there were no changes in the national team from the players Sebes had already been using.

The first half of the year had gone badly for the Golden Squad. After the home defeat against Czechoslovakia and the loss in Belgium, Hungary drew against Portugal away (2–2) then beat Poland comfortably at home (4–1) and Yugoslavia away (3–1), with both Grosics and Czibor restored to the team. Then came a big match at the Lenin Stadium in Moscow.

Puskas: One of the matches we Hungarians were always desperate to win, of course, was any game against the Russians. We drew 0–0 in Moscow in the autumn of 1954, and 1–1 at home later *[September 1955]*. The word in Hungary was that we weren't allowed to win against the Russians, that it was a *political* decision. Well, if it was, no one ever told me about it. Apart from a friendly match in Moscow back in 1950 we had never lost to them, and with Honved we had beaten Dynamo Moscow 3–2 in the opening match at the Nepstadion, and at home as well, 1–0, when I scored a last-minute penalty.

Barcs: We were never warned not to beat the Russians. On the contrary, I remember the Party Secretary coming to the Tata training camp one time before a match against them, and he told the players, 'Score as many as you can. It all remains "in the family".'

Puskas: Anyway, we finally beat the Soviets in Moscow, 1–0, exactly a month before the October Uprising began. But I hadn't realized there were so many people in Hungary who wanted to beat the Russians at more than just football.

8

1956: The Hungarian October Uprising

'It is touching that it was the hooligans of Ferencvaros who created ethics out of nothing during the revolution . . . they were the real heros.'

The build-up

In February 1956, at the Twentieth Congress of the Communist Party of the Soviet Union, Khrushchev delivered the 'secret speech' that denounced Stalin. Slowly, the process of 'rehabilitating' some of the prominent victims of the Russian dictator's murderous purges began in various Eastern bloc countries. That same month, the Hungarian communist Bela Kun – executed in Moscow in 1939 – was rehabilitated, which meant that his innocence was officially recognized and his family could claim his body for a proper burial.

The process of rehabilitating past victims of Stalin's plots and purges threatened many of the old political bosses in Eastern Europe, some of whom were directly implicated in past crimes. In March 1956, the Stalinist dictator of Hungary, Matyas Rakosi, declared that the celebrated Hungarian communist Laszlo Rajk, executed along with other comrades in 1949 as a 'Titoist', had been innocent of all charges. But Rakosi – 'Stalin's best Hungarian disciple' – laid the blame for Rajk's death on the leaders of the state security force, principally Farkas, not upon himself. Calls were nevertheless made for Rakosi's resignation.

In April, more of the remaining political prisoners in Hungary were released and a series of debates amongst writers and intellectuals proceeded, concerning how much further the process of 'de-Stalinization' should go. In June, Laszlo Rajk's widow Julia, who had been campaigning sometimes single-handedly for two years, publicly demanded the rehabilitation of her husband and the prosecution of his murderers. Others demanded the return to power of the ousted Prime Minister Imre Nagy and, as pressure mounted, Rakosi resigned as Party Secretary in July, to be replaced by Erno Gero. Nagy was not yet restored but other 'centrist' politicians like Janos Kadar were brought into the Politburo.

At the same time, in other Eastern bloc countries, the old Stalinists were increasingly destabilized by the new wind blowing from Moscow: the admissions of Stalin's excesses. In Poland, workers' demonstrations in Poznan had to be suppressed by the Polish army. In Hungary, some strikes and disturbances occurred as various groups of workers expressed their general dissatisfaction. By September 1956, numerous critical and inflammatory articles were being published in Hungarian newspapers and journals, attacking the current regime.

The reburial of Rajk

On 6 October, an event took place in Budapest which publicly expressed how deep and widespread the general dissatisfaction was. Rajk's widow had received permission for a ceremonial reburying of her husband's body. It came as Party leaders were preparing for a visit to Yugoslavia and was intended as a goodwill gesture towards

Marshal Tito. They were hoping it would pass off quietly in Budapest, unremarked upon by the general populace. But various influential individuals, from both within and outside the Party, combined to force the leadership to stage a public ceremony with an official funerary oration. The reburial was consequently widely advertised, but even the most optimistic of those opposed to the regime were surprised by the extent of the public response on 6 October:

'On the Sunday afternoon, a march the like of which the city had rarely seen before took to the streets of Budapest. Some put the number as high as 200,000. In the Kerepesi cemetery, where many of Hungary's most famous literary and political figures lie buried, speaker after speaker demanded to know why Laszlo Rajk had died innocent and one of them, a fellow prisoner of Rajk, declared, "We shall not forget!" By the end of the day, members of the opposition, just as much as leaders of the Party, were staggered by the fact that so many people had been so easily mobilized. (Lomax, 1976, p.45)

Within a week, Imre Nagy had been readmitted to the Communist Party. On 21 October, Gomulka was elected First Secretary in Poland despite opposition from Moscow, a development which gave heart to various components of the Hungarian opposition movement. The following day, student meetings in almost all the faculties of Budapest University were in permanent session. The students and staff developed a list of demands, including the withdrawal of Soviet troops from Hungary, a free press and free elections. A mass demonstration was organized, in solidarity with Poland's gesture of independence, for the next day: 23 October 1956. It turned out, accidentally, to be the start of the Hungarian Uprising.

The Uprising: phase one

On Tuesday morning, 23 October, the students sent delegates to leaflet the factories of Budapest, where they received enthusiastic support from the workers. The students, however, refused the offer of a strike in sympathy which would have freed workers to join the demonstration. They were still keen not to provoke the regime and, as yet, there was confusion amongst the senior Party members about whether to sanction the protest. As it was, the Party's own newspaper Szabad Nep *(*Free People*) directly encouraged the students' demonstration in that morning's edition of the paper.*

On the march, the students were joined by thousands of pupils from the city's high schools, and even young officer cadets of the Hungarian Army's 'Petofi Academy' swelled the ranks of the protesters, along with busloads of workers. Later in the morning, the Ministry of the Interior announced a ban on the march, but the students were too far ahead with their plans to take notice. By early afternoon, around 10,000 people had gathered in Petofi Square, bearing Hungarian and Polish national flags and banners proclaiming 'Long Live Polish youth' and 'We trust Imre Nagy'. It was not an 'anti-communist' rally. Some of the students carried a huge portrait of Lenin and sang the socialist anthem, the 'Internationale'.

Petofi's nationalist poem 'Arise Hungarians' was recited and the mood of the crowd shifted as it passed over Stalin Avenue, some calling on workers to smash the huge statue of Stalin. As the march progressed, people returning home from work joined it and after the marchers crossed the Danube to Bem Square, the soldiers from Bem Barracks hung out the Hungarian national flag to greet them. There were many flags being waved now, most of them with the Soviet emblem cut out from where it had been forcibly inserted at the centre of Hungary's national flag. By six o'clock, around a quarter of a million people had gathered in Parliament Square to call for the reinstatement of Imre Nagy at the head of a new, socialist Hungarian government.

Stalin's statue

Other groups headed for Stalin's statue which already had a placard round its neck with a message for the Russian troops: 'Take me with you when you go.' Industrial workers arrived with acetylene torches and cut the great monument off at the knees. Its head was filled with petrol and set alight, flames gushing forth from the old dictator's mouth. Across the city, more crowds had gathered outside the radio station, insisting that their demands be broadcast across Hungary. Instead they got a broadcast from First Secretary Erno Gero, denouncing the demonstrators as 'hooligans' and making no concessions. Inside the station, armed officers of the hated state security force, the AVH, were preparing for the worst.

The first shot that was fired may have been accidental, but once shooting broke out the crowd armed itself and stormed the radio station, shouting, 'Death to the AVH!' By ten o'clock a real battle was in full swing. Word spread through the city that the AVH were shooting at the crowd and soon heavier arms were obtained, sometimes taken, sometimes given to the demonstrators by Hungarian soldiers. That night, the Hungarian government called in Russian troops and tanks to quell the disorder.

The next day, it was announced that Imre Nagy had been appointed Prime Minister. Fighting continued, especially between the crowd and any members of the AVH they could find. On one or two occasions, individual AVH officers were lynched and their corpses hung from lamp-posts, with their salary slips pinned to their lapels (revealing earning of ten to twenty times that of the ordinary worker). Some Russian forces were involved in fighting too, but at first many were confused and sympathetic to the Hungarian people. It was clear to many of the Russians that what was happening was no 'fascist counter-revolution' but a genuine expression of the Hungarian people's desire to change the leadership and direction – but not the fundamental ideology – of their government. On 25 October, however, at a mass fraternization with Russian troops in Parliament Square, somebody – almost certainly the AVH – opened fire with machine guns on the gathered crowd, massacring both Russians and Hungarians. The situation exploded and a period of heavy fighting began, not just in Budapest but across the nation, as the Soviet army sought to stem the revolution.

The football players

The Hungarian Golden Squad was cocooned away from these dramatic events at first, and not just physically.

Puskas: I had no idea what was cooking in Hungary in 1956. This may sound incredible, but we football players lived a charmed life; it was almost a life inside a bubble, protected from the ordinary world, and in which we could live a highly creative existence where we were regularly appreciated and rewarded. Of course, normal people knew something was going to happen, but we weren't 'normal'.

Grosics: We had just played in Belgrade, then Moscow and then in Paris, winning all three matches, and the last stop was Vienna where we beat the Austrians 2–0. We arrived back in Hungary on 22 October and were taken straight to the training camp at Tata. (K&S)

Hidegkuti: On the morning of the 23rd, we were preparing for a game against Sweden, our fifth match in as many weeks. We'd hardly been around Budapest at all for a while.

Grosics: After the late-afternoon training match, somebody happened to switch the radio on. The report indicated that there had been some strange confusion about a particular demonstration in Budapest. First it had been allowed, then prohibited; then suddenly sanctioned again. It was this demonstration – involving tens of thousands of people – which led to the demolition of the great statue of Stalin. The fighting started soon after that.

Hidegkuti: We got a phone call later telling us that there were big demonstrations and it might be that the forthcoming match was in jeopardy. The official who called told us to sit tight and see how things developed. He would keep us informed. Then we got another call at Tata saying that the Sweden match was definitely off and we should all go home.

Barcs: I was in daily contact with the players by phone. I was having big problems with the Sports Ministry by then; they couldn't decide a thing. All decisions had always come from the Party. The Ministry was in effect a telephone exchange, that's all. But the Party was in chaos.

Grosics: We remained for a few more days in Tata, listening to Radio Free Europe because soon no broadcasts were coming from Budapest at all. It was clear that the match with Sweden wasn't going to take place, and everyone was anxious to get home to see that their families were okay. The Budapest train stopped in the suburbs of Buda, at Kelenfold, and we had to walk home from there. The situation in the streets was grotesque: in one place people were cheering and celebrating, while in another they were wounded and dying.

Puskas: I returned to Budapest on 28 October. I think much of the initial fighting had ceased by then. Coming out of the railway station with Cucu Bozsik, it was eerie: no traffic anywhere and I had to make it home on foot, carrying two kilos of bread under my arm. There was no transport and, as I lived in Pest, I had to cross one of the bridges over the Danube. I could hear some shooting in the distance but there wasn't much going on in the centre of town.

Grosics: The league was suspended on the 25th, I think, so I wasn't required to be in Tatabanya. At the time, my family had a house near Gellert Hill – a part of the city that the revolutionaries tried to hold – and I took part in a big demonstration, laying a wreath at the statue of St Imre, before we were fired upon from nearby buildings. Several times

Osterreicher: 'We were carrying money around in paper bags; we had no idea what was going to happen in Hungary.' Puskas stays close to Osterreicher. *(Hungarian Museum of Sport)*

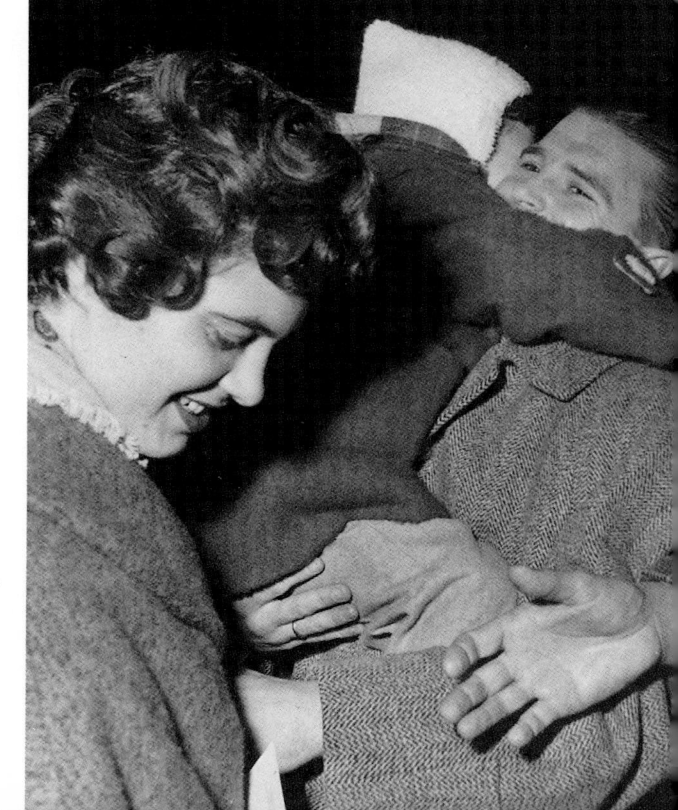

Osterreicher: 'Luckily most of the players' wives had been able to get out.' Puskas reunited with Erzebet and daughter Aniko. *(Popperfoto)*

'At that stage of my footballing life, almost thirty years old, I knew the ban could be tantamount to a virtual death sentence for my career. I might never kick a ball in a serious competition again.' *(Popperfoto)*

Hidegkuti: 'I longed to see Brazil, and I later learned what a good time they'd all had there.' Kocsis, left, and Bozsik on the Brazil tour, 1957. *(Hungarian Museum of Sport)*

'I've always enjoyed his company and his sense of humour.' Puskas and Real Madrid's owner, Santiago Bernabeu. *(Hungarian Museum of Sport)*

An advert for Puskas sausages. *(Hungarian Museum of Sport)*

'My friendship with "Cucu" Bozsik was so close that we were like brothers.' *(Hungarian Museum of Sport)*

'I didn't go back for Bozsik's funeral because I'd sworn never to return to Hungary...' *(Hungarian Museum of Sport)*

The 'Old Boys' game, Budapest, 1981. Tichy: 'He had such a big stomach that we couldn't find a shirt to fit him.' *(Hungarian Museum of Sport)*

Puskas hugs Golden Squad coach Sebes. 'I loved him very much. He was a good friend to my father, and he was like a father to me.' *(Hungarian Museum of Sport)*

'I felt I owed the Spanish people my best, and that's what they got.'
Puskas takes on a regiment of Guards at Wembley, October 1963.
(Popperfoto)

The great carrying the great. Puskas and Yashin lift Stanley Matthews after his testimonial match at Stoke. *(Hungarian Museum of Sport)*

'He weaved a web of charm over this delightful hostess.' Puskas arrives at Speke airport, 1967. Billy Liddell watches in amazement. *(Liverpool Post and Echo)*

'In the end, I will be just an old man who loves football.' *(Hulton Getty)*

revolutionaries came to my place. We gave them food and drink and somewhere to rest, before they went out fighting again. Later, in November, they came and dumped all their weapons there and I had to get rid of them, otherwise I would have been in bad trouble.

Puskas reported dead

In Budapest, confusion reigned and news coming out of Hungary was erratic and suspect. It was announced by the BBC in London (and elsewhere) that Puskas had been killed in the fighting. But in fact, arrangements were already under way which would remove most of the national players from the immediate danger.

Puskas: After the Uprising began, there was an emergency meeting with officials from Honved, who'd had a letter from UEFA warning that failure to play the first leg of our tie against Bilbao (at home) would result in a two-year ban from the new competition, the European Cup, which was then only in its second season. So we arranged to play first in Bilbao and, optimistically, planned the second leg for Budapest in a few weeks time. Getting passports and permissions to go wasn't too much of a hassle – a visit to the Ministry of Defence and the Sports Ministry – and some other sportspeople came along too, table-tennis players I think, whom we got through the border.

The directors of Hungary's 'second' club decided to get that team abroad too.

Hidegkuti: I was at home at first, unable to train at my club MTK. One evening I got a phone call telling me to pack a few things, we were leaving for Austria. I said, 'How are we going to get out? We've no travel documents for a start.' But I was told everything had been arranged. The entire MTK team went to the border in six cars driven in convoy. The 'revolutionary' guards at the border didn't want to let us through because our permits had been issued by the 'old' authorities, but we explained that we had already made commitments to play in Austria and Germany. It was a bit of a lie: we only made the contracts to play some friendlies *after* we arrived in Vienna. The first was against Linz where we won 6–1 in front of a huge crowd.

Puskas: On the last day of October, we went by coach to Vienna. At the Austrian border, some folks did a double-take when they saw me, as the papers had already reported me dead. We spent four days in Vienna before continuing our journey, and it was on our last day there that we heard the news that more Soviet tanks and reinforcements were crossing the borders into Hungary. The Russians weren't about to go home quietly.

The Uprising: phase two

The street fighting in Budapest had continued for five days until, on 29 October, the Soviet forces began to withdraw from the city. Two days earlier, Imre Nagy – the popular choice for Prime Minister – formed a new Hungarian government with some non-communists in the cabinet. Nagy ordered a cease-fire on the 28th and promised that the Soviets would go home and the AVH would be disbanded. On 30 October, the Prime Minister announced the abandonment of the one-party system.

At the start of November, the Hungarian government proclaimed its neutrality and announced its intention to withdraw from the Warsaw Pact. The Hungarian Communist Party was dissolved and one of Nagy's ministers, Janos Kadar, announced the formation of a new party, to be called the Hungarian Socialist Workers' Party. Mysteriously, Kadar then disappeared almost immediately from Budapest.

On 2 November, reports came into the city that Soviet forces were surrounding Hungarian towns and strategic positions, while fresh troops and tank divisions were entering Hungary from Romania and Czechoslovakia in large numbers. The few Stalinists that remained in Nagy's government resigned and a coalition cabinet was assembled. Negotiations with the Russians began about the phased withdrawal of their troops. But at dawn on 4 November, hundreds of Soviet tanks and armoured units entered Budapest in a full-scale attack. Imre Nagy and others sought refuge in the Yugoslav Embassy. Janos Kadar reappeared and announced the formation of a new all-communist government which had requested the Soviet army to assist in restoring order. Heavy fighting raged in towns and cities throughout the country. In parts of Budapest, the Russians were held at bay for more than a week.

The role of the youth

Though the university students – and various groups of writers and intellectuals who formed the 'opposition' in Hungary – had triggered the Uprising, when it came to the fighting it was the industrial workers of Budapest and elsewhere that defended the revolution with such heroic determination. It was in the working-class districts of the capital, especially Ujpest and Csepel (so-called 'Red Csepel'), that the Soviet forces met with the sternest resistance. It was there, too, that the Hungarian mortality rates were at their highest. Miners, steel workers and others arrived from outside Budapest to swell the ranks of the resistance fighters. There were less celebrated heroes too.

'More prominent amongst those who took up the fight against the Russian tanks were the rough, working-class youths of the Budapest slums, the tough guys, the leather-jacketed "yobbos" and hooligans from Angyalfold and Ferencvaros *[districts of Budapest]*. Uncultivated, rude, often anti-semitic, many of them joined for the adventure and sport of the fight. It is with a strange mixture of shame and admiration that the students themselves refer to this development. One of them, for instance, remarks, "It is touching that it was the hooligans of Ferencvaros who created ethics out of nothing during the revolution," and another adds, "Painful as it is to acknowledge it, it is nevertheless true that they were the real heroes." ' (Lomax, 1976, p.111)

The 'Ferencvaros hooligans' were very likely some of those in the Ferencvaros football crowd who had proved so intractable to the regime in the past. Little wonder that Sebes could not even consider the biggest football club in Hungary, with its nationalistic inheritance, as the one to house his Golden Squad.

The Hungarian Uprising was a revolution fought largely by the young, and it was they who were its most immediate casualties. Poverty and hopelessness, rather than any high-flown ideology, were often their motivators. As one young man told a doctor treating him for war wounds, when asked why he was fighting: 'Is it really worth living for six hundred forints a month?'

In Vienna, where the MTK squad was awaiting developments, it was almost impossible to tell what was actually happening in Hungary after the Soviet invasion on 4 November.

Hidegkuti: It was utterly confusing. We were listening to foreign radio stations that people had to translate for us, but every evening at eight o'clock we all sat round to hear the news in Hungarian from Budapest. The situation sounded catastrophic. Austrian television showed scenes of Budapest in ruins, and we were all increasingly worried about family and friends. There was no telephone contact possible until early December, well after we had started to tour and play matches. It wasn't too bad for our families, though. They heard the results given of these games and knew we must all be all right.

There was a director of Ferencvaros in those days called Lajos Onody who was a great sports enthusiast. He was also the boss of a large catering company and he helped my family and many others by supplying food during those very difficult times. He phoned my people every day to make sure they were all right. My wife still says she has never eaten so well since then!

By 11 November, most armed resistance had been crushed by the weight of Soviet tanks and troops. Up to 100,000 Hungarians headed for Austria where the Russians had yet to seal off the border. But resistance did not cease with the fighting. The Workers' Councils which had emerged spontaneously during the revolution remained intact to take on the Soviet-supported Kadar government with the only weapon – though a very effective one – available to them: a general strike. On 21 November, the Central Workers' Council called for a national assembly of delegates to meet in the giant Nepstadion in Budapest. On the morning of the assembly, four hundred Russian tanks surrounded the stadium where the Golden Squad had achieved so many great victories, sealing off all access to it. The Hungarian people were not to be allowed into their 'people's stadium', but the planned meeting went ahead at another location.

A month to the day after the Uprising began, the whole of Budapest went silent for one hour. Not a soul walked the streets; nothing moved. Eleven days later, on 4 December – a month since the second Soviet invasion – a demonstration took place to commemorate those who had lost their lives in the fighting. Despite attempts by Russian tanks and troops to disperse them, a silent procession of Hungarian women, dressed in black and carrying flowers, walked to the Tomb of the Unknown Soldier. As planned, lights were lit in almost every window in Budapest that evening, despite the regime's mean-spirited efforts to withdraw all candles from sale in the city's shops. Soon the reign of terror would begin again.

On tour in Europe

Both Honved and MTK began 'friendly' tours of Europe, raising money from the matches as they went. Both teams were in great demand for prestige games. MTK toured Austria, Germany, Belgium and England. Honved also had a European Cup fixture to play.

Puskas: The Honved party left Vienna for Germany, where we played a couple of friendly matches, principally to raise some ready cash. We had left Hungary in such a rush and didn't really know how long we might be gone. From there it was on to Paris and then to Spain for the European Cup first-leg match versus Bilbao, which we lost 3–2. We played at least three more friendlies, again to raise funds but also to keep match-fit. I think one was in Madrid for a Spanish charity, organized by Franco's wife, and the others were in Italy.

The match in Madrid – a 5–5 draw – was against a selected XI from both of the city's clubs, played on 29 November. Di Stefano played against Puskas's team and the match was watched by Real's owner Santiago Bernabeu. Before leaving Spain, Honved played matches against Barcelona, Seville and Catania during the first few weeks of December. For a while, Grosics was united with his old Honved team colleagues.

Grosics: Towards the end of November, I got a telegram from Spain which said that both of Honved's goalkeepers were injured and the club already had a number of match commitments to keep. Could I join them in Spain? I then got a phone call with instructions: I was to wait outside my house the following day at a given time and transport would arrive. I protested that I had no travel documents, but made plans to take some members of my family with me, at least to Vienna. I didn't recognize anyone in the car that picked us up and it was thoroughly unnerving being followed all the way by Soviet officers in plain clothes. We had to get out short of the border, because there was a tank-trap in the road, and ended up walking over the border where a car met me on the other side. That same day, I arrived in Vienna where an air ticket was waiting; and the next day, I flew to Barcelona and played the same evening.

Osterreicher and the South American tour

Travelling with the Honved party on tour was Emil Osterreicher, the financial secretary of the club between 1954–56. It was his job to organize and arrange the club fixtures.

Osterreicher: 'After the 3–2 defeat against Bilbao we went on tour in Italy, beating Milan 2–1 in the San Siro, amongst other victories. We then travelled to Brussels for the second leg against Bilbao, because it was impossible to play in Budapest. We drew the match 3–3 and went out of the competition.

'We were carrying money around in paper bags; we had no idea what was going to happen in Hungary, but the news wasn't good and we didn't know how long we'd have to survive on the road. While we were in Belgium, we got an offer from the chairman of the Flamengo club in Brazil: $10,000 a match, plus air tickets, to come on tour. This was a great opportunity for the team, many of whom had longed to play in South America, but no one was overjoyed about it because we didn't have permission from the Hungarian FA. We all gathered in the lobby of the Cosmopolitan Hotel to vote on the issue. Bozsik thought we should all go home, but the majority couldn't see the point of returning to the chaos in Budapest. We didn't have any written contract with the Brazilians, but we thought they would keep their word.' (Zsolt, 1989)

Tichy: There were open arguments and rows. The team split into three factions: the first, including Puskas and Czibor, were openly with Osterreicher on this; the second were against, including myself, Budai, and others. The third faction was wavering between the two *[probably including Bozsik and*

Grosics]. The three groups constantly argued about what to do. At one point, on a plane flight, Grosics said, 'I can't wait to go home.' Puskas got really annoyed with him: 'Why did you bother to escape then?' Grosics replied, 'I got out because I love playing football and that wasn't going to be possible at home. It certainly wasn't to travel illegally around the world.'

Meanwhile, the MTK squad had returned to Austria. Sandor Barcs – a long-time supporter of the club and the FA president – offered to go to Vienna and negotiate their return. A little 'sweetener' was offered:

Barcs: I told Party members that I would take the responsibility of getting the MTK squad back to Hungary. They didn't want to return, and I had to call a meeting in Vienna with the whole squad present. I said, 'I am an MTK man; all my life, even during the fascist regime in the thirties when it was thought a "liberal" club, I always supported it.' I told them I had given my word that they would return. I told them the borders would be open; there would be no checks at the customs. Anyway, they came back. I travelled in a car with Hidegkuti, sitting side by side. Altogether we brought thirteen cars through the customs without any controls. Behind the seat of Hidegkuti's car were mountains of luggage.

The only one in the MTK party who didn't return was the man in charge, a director of a huge cartridge factory in Hungary and also an extreme communist. He settled in Germany and is still living there. Funny, isn't it?

Honved – 'the defenders of the homeland' – refuse to return home

On 4 January 1957, reports in Budapest claimed that the Honved team were prepared to return home if the Hungarian FA would give assurances that the South American tour could go ahead at a later date. The FA was already indicating its acquiescence. The

Hungarian FA had applied to FIFA to ban the tour, but FIFA, while 'noting' the Hungarian FA's objections to it announced that it could not ban the tour and informed the associations in Hungary and South America of its decision by letter.

Puskas and Osterreicher gave an interview by telephone to Budapest on 7 January 1957. They stated that the players were now committed to go on the tour. When asked why they wouldn't come home first, they said that the players no longer trusted the authorities who had made promises before which had not been kept. Puskas insisted that everyone would be back home by 31 March, except possibly Czibor who felt he should take up an offer to play in Spain. One of the coaches with Honved, Jeno Kalmar, added, 'I will do my best to get all the players back for the sake of Hungarian football, but at the moment their mood is such that I cannot hold them back.'

Puskas: I have to say that I was never an ideologically committed person, unlike, say, Bozsik to some extent*, or Sebes. I wasn't all that interested in politics, inside the bubble of my football world, playing and training, and leading a happy family life. But obviously I was getting very concerned about developments in Hungary. Luckily, most of the wives of the travelling players had been able to get out during the period when we were away playing the Bilbao matches. I don't know how others organized things; it was all done separately, without too many problems.

Puskas may not have had too many problems getting his wife out, but others did. Some of the players' wives had to be smuggled out in groups by agents employed by Osterreicher in late November. The agents were paid with money the players earned through playing in the prestige matches on the tour. Arguments did develop about Osterreicher's management of these funds and some accused him of slicing money out of the middle.

* Bozsik was, at least nominally, a 'Deputy' of the Hungarian parliament.

Puskas: We contacted Sebes in Hungary and asked for his permission to go to South America. The national coach came to see us with instructions from the FA and the political authorities stating that the proposed tour was not approved and it would be illegal for us to go ahead with it. We said to Sebes (we would address him as 'Uncle' Guszti) that there was no point us going home to face shooting on the streets, and that we wanted to keep playing football. We knew that the league programme had been completely disrupted and wouldn't start up before the spring. He didn't say not to go, but he told us he could not give us permission to go on the tour. We tried again, saying, 'Come with us, and we'll all return home together when things have quietened down,' but he wouldn't hear of it and set off back to Budapest. After some further discussions amongst ourselves, we decided to go to Brazil anyway, and that's what we did.

There was an understandable sense of panic rising in the Sports Ministry in Budapest. Not only were many members of the national team currently abroad – on the Honved tour – but so was the entire under-21 squad, playing in a UEFA competition in Belgium. (In addition, many other world-class Hungarian athletes were much further away in Melbourne, Australia, competing in the 1956 Olympic Games.) Sandor Barcs wrote to Osterreicher.

Barcs: He sent me back a letter with some figures in it, illustrating the kind of money Puskas and the others were earning in Hungary and the kind of money Real Madrid and Barcelona had to offer them. He finished by saying, 'You decide! What should they do?' Well, it wasn't up to me, was it? I showed the letter from Osterreicher to the senior politicians and said, 'I'm sorry, but what can I do?' At least nothing happened to *me*, thank God. You know, in the end we lost over 12,000 registered players. Imagine that!

In December, Sebes was taken to the Hungarian parliament where he was instructed by high-ranking politicians to travel first to Genf in Belgium, where the under-21s were lodged, and then on to meet the Honved party in Brussels, to persuade them all to return home. (Sebes had himself suggested that someone be deputed for this task.)

Barcs: I proposed to the Sports Minister that Sebes be sent to try to get them back. I knew how much the players liked and respected him. They originally wanted to send me, but I couldn't leave Budapest.

Sebes: 'But first, I went to Zurich to see the FIFA executive with a request that no tours or contracts should be sanctioned without permission in advance from the Hungarian FA. I then went to see the juniors in Genf but I didn't get very far in discussions with them. When I arrived in Brussels to see the Honved players on 20 December, I decided not to come on too strong at first. I simply told them how things were developing back home and how everything had calmed down now. I advised them to return after the match against Bilbao and reassured them that they had done no wrong up to now as far as either the Sports Ministry or the Party was concerned. Then they told me about the offer of the South American tour.

'Puskas said: "Uncle Guszti, come with us and lead the team, and I swear we'll all come back home with you afterwards." I must admit it made me think for a few minutes. I had always wanted to go to South America to see where all those brilliant players came from. But in the end I told the boys I couldn't come, I didn't have permission from the Ministry.'

Tichy: Sebes wanted very much to get the Brazil tour approved by the FA. He did everything he could to persuade the Sports Minister to allow it, but he wouldn't give permission. Would you believe, that same guy *[Marcell Bagy]* who refused the permission went to the Olympic Games in Australia a week later and defected himself?

Sebes: 'I watched the 3–3 draw with Bilbao in Brussels – which put Honved out of the competition – and I got the impression that the players didn't really want to win it and go through, because that would have meant a serious re-think of the South American tour. I knew then that I would never again see those great players of the Golden Squad combined in one team.'

9

The Meltdown of the Golden Squad

'It was a terrible wrench to leave so many friends behind in Hungary.'

Most of the Honved party, including Grosics and some other leading players (Lantos and Sandor from MTK and Szusza from Ujpest amongst them), went south to Casablanca to await visas and other arrangements to be made for the South American tour.

Osterreicher: 'Before leaving, we all agreed on the financial arrangements. The players were divided into three groups, from national team players down, and so on. In the end we played seven matches and got $70,000. Puskas got $3,600. But while we were there, he was calling his wife and daughter by phone every day.'

Puskas: The old coach, Bela Guttmann, was living in Vienna at the time we were there before going to Brazil. He had been with Kispest for a while back in the late 1940s, and after periods in

Israel and Portugal he was now in Austria. He was a very experienced and talented coach and we asked him to come to South America with us, which he agreed to do. When we returned to Europe, he remained in Brazil and it was then that he introduced some elements of the 4–2–4 system we had developed, with the two attacking wing-halves interchangeable with the forwards, and the defence pressing up to stay close to the attack.

The Hungarian touring party to Brazil arrived in Rio de Janeiro on 9 January 1957 to a fantastic reception. The players were also very enthusiastic about a trip they had long desired. The Hungarians had planned to tour South America in 1954 after the World Cup, but the 'Battle of Berne' had made that seem unwise. Like Sebes, the Hungarian players saw themselves as the 'Brazilians' of European football (though perhaps it should have been the other way around?) and had longed to visit the country that produced such skilful footballers. The Hungarian party returned to Europe in two separate groups because of visa difficulties, arriving to re-group in Austria around 23 February.

Puskas: After our tour, it was a complicated journey back home to Europe, with half of us coming via the Netherlands and half through Spain. In the end, we all met up again in Vienna. Various authorities were dispatched from Budapest to meet with us, and a 'trial' was held in Vienna; we were told we all had to come back to Hungary right away to face various 'punishments', the most severe being reserved for me as captain. (I said, 'Why me? If I'm the one who decides which side of the coin to call, so what?') After some heated argument, I told them to find out from the FA precisely what they meant by 'punishments' and to call me the next day. I was then informed that I was to be banned from playing football for eighteen months.

Vandor: It was all the fault of the new president of the Hungarian FA who'd been put in place of Sandor Barcs. His name was Marton Nagy. He fancied himself as a 'hard man' and felt he had to put on a tough show to impress the Soviets: 'If they're not back within forty-eight hours, they're all banned.' That's why they didn't return. I have longed to meet Nagy ever since, to knock his block off. It was a terrible message to send to our greatest players.

Offers from abroad

While Honved and MTK had been travelling abroad, offers had been raining in for various players of both teams, especially for those who were members of the Golden Squad. Spanish and Italian clubs were particularly keen to keep track of developments. Lajos Tichy, the centre-forward at Honved, returned to Budapest before the rest left for South America and gave an account of what had happened before the first match against Bilbao.

Tichy: We hadn't even had time to unpack our suitcases before we were surrounded by agents. There wasn't a single player who didn't get an offer of some kind. Kocsis and Czibor got the best offers, around $120,000 each. I don't know how much Bozsik was offered.

Hidgekuti and most of the MTK party had returned to Budapest before Christmas. They too had been targeted by agents from various countries.

Hidegkuti: We got many offers while touring abroad. But my situation was that I had a wife and two kids at home; my wife's parents were there too, and her father had just had to have his leg amputated. There was no way I could leave Hungary. I was the sole support for these people.

I did have serious thoughts about the South American tour, though. My MTK team-mate Sandor phoned from Vienna to tell me about it, but by then the borders were effectively closed. It was just about impossible to get out under those circumstances and quite a risk even to attempt it. So I stayed put. I did think, though, that quite a number of players might defect over there and knew that my heart would break if I was faced with the choice of staying with my mates or returning home. But I hated to miss out on that South American tour. I longed to see Brazil, and I learned later what a good time they'd all had there. Anyway, I missed out on that one. I told Sandor afterwards that if he'd called me earlier, I'd have stayed in Vienna and gone direct from there to Brazil. After all, the Brazilians were the other great football team in the world, weren't they?

Puskas and Bozsik

In Vienna, after the visit from the Hungarian FA officials, Puskas and others took their separate decisions. The situation between Bozsik and Puskas was a poignant one. Here were two close friends since early childhood, whose football had blossomed in an almost symbiotic partnership to reach the greatest heights in the world game. They had played together in the same teams all their shared lives, since those barefoot games in Kispest a quarter of a century previously. But these friends were two very different personalities, now facing in two utterly opposed directions. Bozsik – thoughtful, introverted, a Party member and Hungarian parliamentary Deputy – was going home; Puskas – always the rebel, spontaneous, extroverted, egotistical – was going elsewhere.

Puskas: We didn't try to persuade each other about staying or going. We knew each other's situation and it needed no explanation from either of us. For me, it was relatively simple. My wife and daughter were with me in Vienna. Cucu and I spent many days together there before he returned to Budapest. He had a lot of doubts about going home, and for a while he was close to staying in the West*, but his mother and four brothers were in Hungary and he'd recently lost his father. I think he felt he just had to go home, but he did it without much enthusiasm. You must remember that we were then high-ranking officers in the Hungarian Army, which meant we were technically 'deserters' if we didn't go back. That put us under considerable pressure.

At the final meeting with Hungarian FA officials in Vienna, I gave them an ultimatum: if they changed their minds about the ban, I would return; if not, I was on my way. I told them to go back to the Sports Minister and ask again. By the time I received their reply – in the negative – Kocsis and Czibor had already left Austria, one to Italy *[Czibor]*, the other to Switzerland. They had decided a day earlier.

At that stage of my footballing life, almost thirty years old, I felt the ban was a virtual death-sentence for my career. I might never kick a ball in serious competition again. I told them, I'm sorry but no thanks, goodbye. That's how I left them, and a few days later I flew with my wife and family to Italy.

Things did not look good for Puskas. The Hungarian FA sought to extend its domestic ban through FIFA, so that the players abroad could not play professionally. Yet Kocsis soon went to Barcelona and was joined there by Czibor after the Italian FA had refused to allow the latter to sign for Roma. They both took up their playing careers again with considerable success after serving out their one-year ban. But Puskas received few offers and those that came were often not to his liking.

Tichy: I was surprised that Puskas didn't get any good offers. He got one from Portugal inviting him to be a coach there. He was fuming. 'I'm not old enough to be a coach yet,' he raged, 'I want to play.'

* Osterreicher had fixed up a coaching job for Bozsik at Atletico Madrid.

Puskas: As it worked out, the career situation looked even worse for me than if I had gone back to Budapest. I had left my club, Honved, without permission, making me nothing more than an amateur, unable to play professionally for a year. Then the Hungarian FA asked FIFA for an additional one-year ban. So that was two years out. Some Italian clubs were still interested in me and eventually an application was made to FIFA to rescind the ban. In the end, they knocked six months off and agreed to count the period from the second Bilbao match *[i.e. 19 January 1957 to 19 July 1958].*

Puskas's decision not to return home reverberated through the Hungarian football world. He had received a few very generous offers in the past which he had always refused. Some of his closest colleagues found it hard to believe that he wouldn't be returning to Budapest.

Hidgekuti: I wasn't surprised Czibor stayed in the West. His life was always chaotic and I think he'd even taken a public part in some of the anti-Soviet demonstrations. So we all expected him to stay away. Kocsis was a bit of a surprise, but I don't think he was married at the time and so he was free to go in that sense. But I didn't expect Puskas to remain abroad. We all thought he'd come back home in the end. Even today, I don't really know why he stayed in the West.

Grosics: I knew some would never return home. In practice, it was the end of the era of the Golden Squad. Players like Puskas, Kocsis and Czibor were in truth irreplaceable, not only then but ever since. When 'Ocsi' didn't return in the spring of 1957, I was sure Hungary would never have such a great team again.

An offer from Real Madrid

Puskas: It worked out that I was banned for thirteen months from the moment I arrived in Italy. I was beginning to get more confident that someone would sign me when I became available. Inter Milan soon made me an offer and I began to join their squad for training (which I did for about three months), but I had got quite fat – eighteen kilos overweight. About two months before the ban was due to be rescinded, Inter told me they wouldn't be able to sign me because their FA required them to register their players at a given date, and I couldn't be registered because I wasn't officially available yet.

Barcs: I still have a letter today from Puskas. It is dated 5 October 1957. It asks me to try to free him from the ban so he can be registered with a club. Of course, there was nothing I could do for him. It was a Party decision.

Puskas: At this point I began to panic a bit about what the future might bring. The months of being banned had been depressing, only bearable because the prospect of joining Inter seemed good. I couldn't even step on a proper football pitch and I wasn't supposed to visit any professional training ground. During those first few months in Bordighera, Italy, there was a small local club in San Remo whose players trained in the afternoon, so I could go there alone in the mornings. After the collapse of the Inter offer, I didn't entirely give up hope but when I heard from Emil Osterreicher that the owner of Real Madrid, Santiago Bernabeu, wanted to see me, I was delighted.

When Osterreicher had arrived back in Vienna from Brazil, he had decided not to face the 'punishments' waiting back in Hungary either, and had left for Spain where he eventually got a job at Real Madrid. Osterreicher had met Bernabeu when Honved played the 'Select XI' from Madrid in December 1956, and the owner of Real invited him to join the club as 'technical director'.

Osterreicher: 'My first job was to locate and suggest players to strengthen the squad. Of course, I was already thinking about Puskas but Bernabeu didn't seem keen – he had seen him play in that match in Madrid and hadn't been impressed, and he also thought Puskas argued too much with referees. So I just sat on the idea for a while. Finally, after Inter failed to sign him, Bernabeu agreed that I should contact Puskas. We met up in Bologna.'

Puskas: Osterreicher was in Italy to cast his eyes over AC Milan, who Real Madrid were to meet (and beat) in the European Cup Final that year. He said that Bernabeu wanted me to play for the European champions. I said, 'I'm too fat, I can't possibly play. I need time to get my weight down.' He said don't bother about that, get on the plane and come with me. So there I was the next day in Madrid, the size of a large balloon, having a very weird 'conversation' with Bernabeu. There was no interpreter present. He was rabbiting away in Spanish; me in Hungarian. He then tried a bit of German and I responded in the few words of Spanish I knew. In the end, I threw up my arms and gestured, 'Listen, this is all very well but have you looked at me? I'm at least eighteen kilos overweight.' Bernabeu replied, 'That's not my problem, it's yours.' And that was that. I was a Real Madrid player, if a rather heavy one.

Osterreicher: 'For a four-year contract Puskas got nearly $100,000, paid in Spanish currency, plus wages and bonuses. It wasn't much to pay for a fit Puskas, but it wasn't bad for a fat one.'

Puskas: Bernabeu gave me $5,000 immediately, which came in very handy. I flew back to my family in Italy and told them the news. We packed and left for Vienna first, where we had left some of our things, and from there it was a flight to Madrid. I got down to work – hard work – and lost those eighteen kilos in just six weeks. It was one hell of an effort but I knew it would be worth it. So it was no bread, no alcohol at all, and I told my wife I didn't even want to *see* a plate of spaghetti.

Szepesi: I think if Puskas had returned to Hungary in 1956, his career would have been over. He was fat, unfit and nearly thirty. I was really surprised he got another ten years at Real Madrid. He needed the enormous challenge that Spain presented. At home he could relax, 'vanish' from a match, do what he wanted. He was under no pressure. It wasn't like that at Real.

Sandor Barcs encountered Puskas in Spain. It was a revealing experience.

Barcs: We went to lunch in Madrid sometime in 1958. Puskas ordered a kind of seafood, something I'd never seen before. He ordered it for me, too, and I couldn't eat it. I said, 'Ocsi, what is this stuff? What are you eating these days, for God's sake?' He just smiled at me and said, 'I'm a *professional* now, you know.'

The decline of Honved

Without three of their great players, Honved struggled in the season that followed the defection of Puskas, Czibor and Kocsis. The club would have been relegated, but the authorities saved it from such a fate by deciding to enlarge the first division. Some say Bozsik and others were detained and questioned for days after their return – and Bozsik received a six-month ban – but others insist that nothing happened to Bozsik. Predictably, Grosics got the most unfriendly welcoming party.

Grosics: On my return home in May that year, they met me at the border with a prison van. The shadow of suspicion never really dissipated. In the archives of the AVH, I was an unreliable character who needed special attention. Even nowadays, I wonder whether I did the right thing to come back home. I still don't know.

Hidegkuti: Honved attempted to compensate for the loss of Puskas and others by drafting in more youngsters, 'conscripting' them into the army team. But over the coming years, Honved did eventually decline as players got more freedom to choose their own clubs and the political bosses at other clubs refused to give up their best players to the 'army'. Of course, the loss of Puskas, Kocsis and Czibor in the national team was huge, and we also lost the whole of the under-21 squad who had defected too. That's how we lost so much of our footballing strength so fast. My generation was getting old anyway, but the cream of the youth went as well.

In Hungary, the Kadar regime had finished pussy-footing around with the Workers' Councils and any other form of opposition. Early in 1957, the death penalty was extended to workers going on strike or inciting strikes. Soon the AVH was re-formed and the death penalty extended to encompass virtually any act of criticism of the regime.

Puskas: The only close family left to me in Budapest was my mother and my sister. They lived in the house I had bought in the city and I knew they could look after the place and themselves too, if necessary. They were both strong characters, very competent women, and they managed very well indeed. In the end, of course, my friend Bozsik returned to Budapest, even though his wife had made it out of Hungary. So they could have left together – but she went back and Bozsik followed. That was their decision. Little did I realize that I would never see my friend on Hungarian soil again.

Manchester United

On 6 February 1958, the city of Manchester – and much of Britain – went into mourning. In the Munich aircrash, Manchester United lost seven players, including Duncan Edwards, Tommy Taylor, Roger Byrne and David Pegg – all internationals.

Puskas: During the ban, which affected Czibor, Kocsis and myself, Manchester United applied to FIFA to 'borrow' all three of us until the ban expired. They were desperately short of players after the terrible accident at Munich. The club proposed to pay us a basic wage and so on, but neither FIFA nor the English FA would allow it, although it took them about six weeks of arguing to decide. In the end, it was some legal reason that prevented it.

Of course, Real Madrid played Manchester in the European Cup semi-final the year before *[in 1957, Real winning the home leg 3–1 and drawing at Old Trafford 2–2]* – and would probably have played them in the Final a year later if it hadn't been for that dreadful air crash. I was in Italy when I heard the news, about ten minutes after it happened. The shock was tremendous, only relieved a little when we heard that Matt Busby and Bobby Charlton had survived. I liked Busby a lot. He was a great football man. All of us football players realized that it could easily have been any of us in a plane like that. Manchester United were just becoming a very good side. Duncan Edwards was stunning to watch, so young yet with such power. He was a massive physical presence on the pitch, always working for the team. A great loss to the club and the game as well. Sometime after the crash, when I was playing for Real, we travelled to England to play a friendly against United at Old Trafford to help raise money. We beat them 6–1.

Uncle Guszti

Puskas: It was a terrible wrench to leave behind so many friends in Hungary, especially the coach who had nurtured my international career. Sebes was a very intelligent, calm and fundamentally good man. He was fair-minded and never hurt anyone; always ready to help, if he could, those who asked for his help. He was respected enormously by all the players. The truth is he *loved* us – not just me and Bozsik but all of us in the Golden Squad. He was one of the most genuine and honest people I've ever known and, looking back, there is nothing I could find to say against him.

He was a good international player in his youth. After the war, when he became national coach – and also Deputy Minister at the Sports Ministry – he was the real head and heart of that golden team. He was a serious man, very professional, but he had a real sense of humour and we did have a lot of fun in his company. We loved telling jokes about him, needless to say, but I tell you he knew our very souls, knew what we needed to succeed, and made sure we got it.

He was, of course, a committed communist and he never lost that faith. His role in the creation of the Golden Squad was central, but things got a little difficult for him after the 1956 Uprising and the subsequent loss of players like Kocsis, Czibor and myself. There was a search for scapegoats afterwards and Sebes suffered somewhat, and it was that which held Hungarian football back from further improvements. In addition, quite a few youngsters who'd got out refused to return home after 1956 and many of their coaches back in Budapest got very disheartened. The Golden Squad players, like me, were all getting on a bit too, and it needed fresh supplies of young talent to keep going at that standard. Despite the presence of Grosics, Buzanszky, Budai, Bozsik and Hidegkuti in the team which went to the 1958 World Cup, they didn't look anywhere near the old team. And by then they had lost Sebes, dismissed the year before from his posts as national coach and Deputy Sports Minister.

Sebes resigned his post at the Ministry in January 1957, claiming that it had become impossible for him to work there any longer. He went on to coach at Ujpest and Honved in the years that followed, and many recognized him as the father of 'total football'. But his greatest creation was the Golden Squad. He had built it principally around Puskas, and without him it could not stand.

Hidegkuti: When Puskas left the country, the national team was never the same again. I often played in his position afterwards but I couldn't make up for his absence. He was not only a great player and captain, but also a 'playing coach'. He saw everything, exerted great discipline over the whole team, and could analyse footballing situations on the run. A few brief instructions on the field from him and all our problems were solved.

10

The Real Madrid Years, 1958–67

Part One

'The coach said I wasn't good enough playing in the mud.'

Many people, both inside and outside the game, thought Puskas was probably finished as a player, at least as a great player. When he arrived in Madrid he was thirty-one years old, well out of condition, and hadn't kicked a ball in earnest for nearly two years. Real Madrid looked like a difficult club to join too, especially for someone used to being a captain and having a major influence on team affairs. At Real, Alfredo Di Stefano, arguably the world's greatest player at the time, was the boss on the field, and many Real fans off it were sceptical about Puskas's fitness and ability to 'gel' with their great star. Once the season started, the supporters thought him slow and ponderous at first, and indeed the Spanish league game was *faster than the Hungarian style of 'making only the ball travel quickly'. But Puskas needed match practice most of all, and he ended up second top-scorer (one goal behind Di Stefano) in the Spanish league that season, 1958–59.*

Puskas: I arrived in Madrid in the summer of 1958, a couple of months before the new season kicked off. I joined the squad for six weeks' training and then we all went off to Argentina – I made my debut for Real Madrid in Buenos Aires – before going on to Uruguay, and we returned to Spain just in time to start the season. The first league match I played in *[against Oviedo on 2 September]* we won 5–2, and I got a couple of goals, one with my head which wasn't easy as the pitch was soaking and you could hardly get off the ground. But I loved the atmosphere in the stadium, which had 100,000 fans inside despite the rain.

We got a good press after the game but when it came to the next fixture – away to San Sebastian – the coach, Carniglia, took me aside before leaving and said, 'I'm leaving you out of this one because the ground is heavy and wet again, and I know you don't like that.' I said, okay. What else can a new player do? It was a nil-nil draw and, on the way back, the chairman, Bernabeu, asked me why I hadn't played. I said something to the effect that only eleven can play and the coach said I wasn't good enough playing in the mud, so he rested me. The chairman said nothing but I was in the team next week.

Osterreicher: 'Carniglia didn't like Puskas from the moment he arrived. Of course, he wasn't in condition and, even after the league kicked off, for a while Puskas was simply running while the others were playing. But he just got his head down and got stuck in. Soon the other players – a little distant at first – began to get on very well with him, and Bernabeu got to like him very quickly too.'

Puskas: The Spanish league was a fair bit quicker than I was used to, and more competitive as well. It wasn't like Honved and MTK in a division which one of them was bound to win. But I gave no thought to that, just determined to try my very best and succeed. I was probably more determined than at any time in my life. I knew I couldn't expect the same service I had been used to at Honved and for Hungary, and I didn't get it. There was no Bozsik who'd played with me since I was three years old and to whom I only had to say 'Now, Cucu' to get the required pass in the perfect place.

At first, I hardly knew anyone at the club. I'd only spoken to players on the pitch, and not much of that because my Spanish didn't really extend beyond 'Buenos dias' and 'Buenas noches'. I couldn't manage a conversation at all. It took me at least six months to get a grip on it; my wife learned the language as well and my young daughter, playing with Spanish kids all the time, got it in no time at all. I bought a beautiful house about three kilometres from the stadium. The club paid wages and bonuses but I paid for my own house.

I took up the same inside-left position that I had played in Hungary and did my best to complement the rest of the team. I got 21 goals that season and Di Stefano 22, but after that I was the Spanish league's top scorer four years on the trot. My game was different but I adjusted to theirs quickly. If Gento got the ball on the left wing, I soon learnt that he was so quick that if I didn't hit top speed instantly, there would be no one there when he crossed the ball. And of course I had to find my game in amongst some of the greatest players in the world at the time, Di Stefano, Kopa, Rial and so on.

Real Madrid had not always been the giants they were becoming when Puskas joined them. Santiago Bernabeu got involved in 1943 when the stadium held a mere 16,000 and Real were very much a second-rate team. It was Bernabeu who totally reorganized the club and built the new stadium, with money partly raised by a membership scheme which provided 'shares' in the football club. Members could use the other facilities – pools, tennis courts, gym, even a hospital – at the site. Real became the model European club, with a state-of-the-art stadium and a team to match. They won the European Cup for the first five consecutive years of the competition.

Puskas: Soon the 100,000 fans packed into the Bernabeu Stadium every week were my best friends. They really got to love me but I honestly believe I deserved it. During my time there, along with the European Cup victories, we won many honours including five consecutive league titles from 1960 to 1961 onwards, an unequalled feat in Spanish football. I never let those fans down and gave my best to them whenever possible. I really felt surrounded by their affection and respect, which is no doubt why I had such a good life in Spain and still have so many warm memories of that time.

Back in Hungary

After 1956, Puskas had gone from national hero to virtual 'non-person' in his home country. There was very little official news in Hungary about his developing career in Spain, except that which travelled along the footballing grapevine.

Tichy: When Puskas started playing for Real we heard little more than the results of their matches. You see, the political leaders were blamed by the people for driving him and others out of Hungary. So nobody was allowed to mention them. Of course we were all desperate to hear news of Puskas especially and we grabbed every morsel we could find. We heard the rumours that he'd lost weight and we were dying to know how well he was playing.

Alfredo Di Stefano

The challenges Puskas faced in Madrid should not be underestimated. In addition to his difficulties reaching the right physical condition (and his encroaching years made that even harder), he needed the right mental attitude too. Puskas had run just about every team he had played in, almost from his teenage years onwards. He had captained Honved, the most powerful club in the land, and Hungary, the best national side in the world. He led those teams on to the pitch; he structured the on-field tactics; he often virtually selected the side and, as Tichy said, 'If Puskas wanted stew, that's what we got.'

At Real Madrid, he was joining a team with someone already firmly occupying the elevated position that Puskas had held all his footballing life. In Madrid, Di Stefano was the great star, captain and leader of his men. It was he who ran out on to the pitch first, dominated the life of the club and attracted the main focus of attention. It could very easily have gone all wrong for Puskas in Spain, but he showed a very sharp intelligence and a diamond-hard determination to succeed. Wisely, he did not try to compete with Di Stefano. He watched and listened, studying the great Argentinian player until he felt he understood him.

Puskas: Despite what might have looked like a difficult situation from the outside, I never had any real problems with Di Stefano. Of course in Hungary, for club and country, I was used to running out on to the pitch first, as captain, so in Madrid I completely reversed that and made it a tradition that I came out last. When I arrived there, I studied Di Stefano intensely and got to know him as quick as I could, both as a player and as a person.

Osterreicher: 'In the last match of that first season, Puskas and Di Stefano were equal as top goalscorers in the league. It was against Granada and Real were on the attack. Puskas had the ball at his feet – and the goal at his mercy – when he laid it off to Di Stefano, to let him score.'

Puskas: We were equal on twenty-one goals each. I thought to myself, if I score here, he'll never speak to me again. It was the best way. He was the season's top scorer and I was second. We became firm friends.

Di Stefano's not the easiest of men, even today, and he could be a touch unpredictable. But I'll tell you what dominated his life: the enormous desire to *win* and to be the best at any cost. If that was threatened, he could be as stubborn and merciless as a young child. He was just as ruthless with himself, and if his own form wasn't quite there – it can happen to anyone – he would make up for it with energy and enthusiasm, and sheer effort if necessary. And he wanted the same from everyone else. He didn't like strangers and if any approached he would clam up and appear very unfriendly, but if someone he knew introduced a person to him, a friend, a supporter or anyone, he was charming and hospitable.

Didi

In the summer of 1959, Real brought the Brazilian midfielder Didi (Valdir Pereira), from Botafogo. It was at a previous club, Fluminense, in the early 1950s that Didi had perfected the 'banana' kick, bending the ball round a wall of players into the net. He was the star of Brazil's 1958 World Cup winning team and wore the title 'world's best player', which was never going to warm him to Di Stefano's heart. There were rumours of a 'personality clash' between the new Brazilian and Real's Argentinian captain. In the event, Didi didn't last long at the club.

Puskas: When Didi lost his place in the Real team, many put it down to Di Stefano's criticism but I don't think he had much to do with it. Didi was a skinny little thing when he arrived at Madrid and he could really shift. He was only at the club for about eighteen months and I'm afraid he got fat and slow; he seemed to have put on the kilos I had taken off! And a slow player had no chance in that side.

Didi was at first loaned to Valencia then sold back to Botafogo in

1960. He left claiming that Di Stefano had instituted a 'boycott' against him in 'a determined campaign' to destabilize his position at Real.

Puskas: Di Stefano didn't tell players off on the field, although you could sometimes hear him grumbling away and we'd grumble right back. In some ways, it wasn't so different from the way things were at Honved – there were no big recriminations in the dressing-room after a match – but perhaps we were firmer friends in Hungary. There, we had, after all, known one another since our teens and grown up together in many ways.

Di Stefano, anyway, had a right to grumble if he wanted: he was a great player and saw things others didn't see. No game is perfect, there are always mistakes, and Di Stefano would have a list of them in his head at the end: so-and-so didn't move into space quick enough; somebody should have seen him in the position he had found, but where was the pass? I never minded. He was perhaps the greatest centre-forward in the world at the time. He knew the game back to front and was always physically and mentally well-prepared. I think I made a small contribution to his game: he liked to lie very deep, almost in defence, and sometimes found it too much to get forward into the attack. I encouraged him to assume a position further forward, very similar to Hidegkuti's in the Hungarian deep-lying centre-forward role, and like that we scored a hell of a lot of goals between us. He was by no means unapproachable in that sense. Alfredo and I were good friends then and we are the same today. He still calls me 'Pancho'.

We spent a week together quite recently at the World Cup in the USA (1994). A great deal of rubbish has been written about him, about how cold and distant he appeared to those who didn't know him. But I know what he went through. That kind of fame could be a real burden, even back in those days when the media wasn't as crazy as it is today. After a while, I understood what

Alfredo was going through. I tried very hard to remain approachable, be the 'good boy' always affable and smiling. But some people out there can be really obnoxious.

The pre-match Real routine

Puskas: In Spain, of course, matches were played on Sundays. On the Friday night before an away game, we would travel to the host city or hide away in a hotel somewhere en route. For home matches, it was always up to our regular place, a kind of holiday resort forty kilometres from Madrid, in the mountains. We had a great time there. It was very relaxed; the food was excellent and everything was there that you might need. The club was undoubtedly the foremost in Europe – perhaps even the world – at the time, and the organization was superb. I was very careful to behave well and not to get up anyone's nose by playing the 'superstar'. There were many stars in that team.

On the Saturday evening, the coach would visit everyone. There were two players to a room, and round he would come with a few words about tomorrow's opponents; try to take care of so-and-so, try to do this, etc. It took five minutes at most. In the dressing-room immediately prior to the game, the same instructions would be briefly repeated and that was it. We got on with it. There was perhaps just a bit more talk than I was used to at Honved, but there we knew every opposing Hungarian player and his father too. After a few months in Spain, I soon got to know who could do what amongst our opponents. Our game was fairly simple: we knew that in Gento we had the quickest thing on two legs down the left wing; Alfredo would start moves from deep and get it wide if he could; I was up front with Rial, and Kopa was wide on the right. Mateos took over that role and Del Sol came after him. That changed the shape a little; there were virtually two 'lying deep' then. Di Stefano's game was more energetic than Hidegkuti's: he ran more than 'Nandi' ever did, and really covered the ground.

Gento

Francisco Gento was the fastest winger in Europe with a fine footballing brain to match his speed. He won six European Cup medals during a stunning eighty-eight appearances in the competition, eventually captaining Real (after Di Stefano) and Spain. His career began in 1952; he joined Real in '53, and he was still playing for them in the European Cup-Winners Cup Final (against Chelsea) in 1971.

Puskas: Gento is still a very good friend. As players, we shared rooms for nine years whenever we travelled with the club. He still likes to tell the story about how he would throw me the soap in the showers and I would catch it with my left foot and keep it up for a while. It's true.

He was slightly strange-looking, small with dark curly hair, and very quiet. He came to Real from Santander before my arrival and I believe he had a pretty rough ride at first, although there were no problems after I got there. Apart from his amazing quickness, he had a superb touch on the ball. We taught each other a lot, practising moves together in training. I used to say, 'Paco, hit the ball to my feet. If you make me run too much, I'll get tired.' There was a lot of joking around. He had a tremendous shot but it could be wildly inaccurate sometimes, disturbing the birds in the trees round the training ground, and we could never find the ball afterwards. He is a lovely guy, once a great player, and still does something at the club even today.

When I compare him with that other great left-winger I've played with, Czibor, I have to say that Gento was probably the more consistently dangerous attacker. But Czibor took life less seriously and I could understand him easier. He was a less stable personality – unpredictability was part of his charm – and in that

Hungarian team he could afford to allow himself more freedom.

Life in Madrid

Nobody ever made me feel a 'foreigner' in Madrid and I never felt it necessary to jettison my Hungarian-ness; not that I could. Neither would I criticize my homeland. I made friends with Hungarians who lived in Madrid, or people came to visit me from home. But the media commentators never mentioned my nationality at all. I played fair with everyone and got back as good as I gave.

But at first I did consciously try to forget about Hungary. It was too painful to recall that so many of my good friends were still there in an unpredictable situation. I knew I had to make a new life in Spain – learn the language and carve out a place for myself in the team – and that took all the concentration and determination I could raise. So for a while, I avoided reading the Hungarian sports results, or any news from home really, to avoid the longing and the distraction. It took about three or four years really, before I could relax about it and, if a Hungarian sports team was in town, go out to see them and have a chat. That was the point at which I began to reconnect with what was happening in Hungarian sport.

After the Hungarian Uprising and the defection of around 100,000 citizens, there were pockets of expatriate Hungarians in cities all over Europe.

Puskas: Almost everywhere I went with the Real team, there were always little groups of Hungarians waiting to welcome me. They identified with me as one who, like them, had been unable to remain after 1956. As the team took to the pitch in various European countries, sometimes I could even hear the shout, 'Hat harom' which means 'six three' – a reference to that great game at Wembley in 1953. Of course, it made me feel good to hear them but, inevitably, I found myself in the role of 'interpreter', having to introduce the whole team to these little groups and say a few words about each player. The rest of the team would get fed up with it, saying, 'Come on, we could be here until morning at this rate.'

I had to sign thousands of photographs, flags, shirts, any old scrap of paper, throughout a season, and I had to lean on the other players to follow me. I think they often found it a bore; these people were complete strangers to them. But of course these folks looked to me to help them. Many of them had grown up watching me play for Honved or Hungary, and I did do my best to remember that. Sometimes it wasn't easy. Sometimes I felt I had had enough, but how can one ignore a fellow countryman after a history like ours? How could one ignore being addressed in Hungarian? Regardless of how tired I was, it wouldn't be human to walk past.

I could keep in touch – by letter and phone – with friends and relatives in Hungary, although with my mum it was almost exclusively by phone because her eyesight was getting poor and she said she couldn't read my writing any longer. But I sent her postcards from all over the world and she was able to come to Madrid – and later to Greece – and stay sometimes with me and the family. She was a very genuine, hard-working, down-to-earth woman and I loved her very much.

Problems with coach Carniglia

Puskas: It had been a bit unnerving being dropped for that second match. I never felt entirely comfortable with Carniglia and it all came to a head in 1959, at the end of my first season, when we played Reims in the European Cup Final in Stuttgart. But before that, there had been a series of gripping matches in the semi-final against Real's great rivals, Atletico Madrid. I scored in the first game from a penalty. I hadn't played particularly well, but neither had quite a few others. A fortnight later we met again; another draw, so a third match was played and I got the winner (with my right foot, too). There had been rumours that I would be dropped for the second match, but I ignored them.

I played another league game versus Bilbao before we were off to Stuttgart for the final. The coach hadn't said anything to me at all during the few days' training in Germany, but an hour before the game he came over and told me I was 'injured' and wouldn't be playing. There was little I could do about it. The coach thought I wasn't fit and, in those days, there were no substitutes. I was very down about it. It would have been my first European Cup Final (and no one knew we would be there again the following year). But I've never been a sulker, and I watched the match from the stands. Real played well and won 2–0. We got a penalty too (I normally took the spot-kicks) and my replacement missed it. After the match, the club directors were congratulating all the players, and the chairman sat down next to me and asked why I didn't play. I explained that Carniglia had told me I was 'injured'. Did you get a knock in training? I said that I thought I was fine but he had better ask the coach himself.

Anyway, we all went back to Madrid and off on a thirty-day break from football. At our first day training, there was the chairman in the dressing-room shaking everyone's hand and asking how we were. He didn't say another thing, but returned to his office and wrote a note to Carniglia saying thank you for your work with the club but your contract is not being renewed. That was it; no one was told about it, we just heard later. I'm convinced that Carniglia's unpredictable attitude towards me cost him the job. I don't think Bernabeu liked Carniglia very much, despite the team's success. Carniglia was a rather strange guy but, many years later, I got on quite good terms with him.

In fact, while going through some old photographs, I discovered to my amazement that I had actually played against him on that 1947 Ferencvaros tour to Mexico. He did seem somehow familiar when I met him in Madrid in 1958, but I had never realized what it was. And he had never mentioned it while he was Real's coach.

11

The Real Madrid Years, 1958–67

Part Two

'It was fantastic to be involved in another Golden Squad.'

Real Madrid became the best club side in the world. The addition of Puskas to a team that already included Di Stefano, Kopa, Gento and Santamaria seemed to raise Real's game to a sublime level. Its greatest flowering occurred at the 1960 European Cup Final in Glasgow, a game which many observers felt – and still feel – was the finest European club match of all time. Puskas was, of course, only a part of that team, but the fact is that his presence seemed to catalyse the achievement of some kind of footballing perfection. This was not a unique event in his life, rather the opposite. Every single team Puskas played for, from Honved through Hungary to Real Madrid, was arguably the greatest side in the world while he played for them. This is one of the features of his life which lifts Puskas into the sphere of the most truly remarkable footballers. Virtually his entire playing career – over twenty years – was spent not just at the top but at the very top *of his profession. He never stepped down from that summit. Almost whatever he touched in the footballing world turned to gold.*

Puskas: It was fantastic to be involved in another Golden Squad. There was real camaraderie in that Real team – perhaps not quite as close as at Honved, but that was understandable. For a really great team, I think genuinely close human relationships are essential. At least they have been in my life. The foreigners in that Real team got on with each other particularly well. Kopa – of French/Polish extraction – Alfredo and myself formed the card school when travelling and we would clean up against the Spanish players, who weren't as good as us. Kopa had a great sense of humour, but Alfredo would rage if he lost at cards (and he would only bet the smallest Spanish currency he could find).

Even when younger players arrived at the club, they joined the company easily and we 'old boys' – ten or twelve years older than some of these lads – did our best to relax them and make them feel at home. Wives and girlfriends were encouraged to get to know one another, to sit together to watch the matches and so on. Once a month players and families would gather socially, which gave more opportunities for friendship. There was virtually no gossiping or back-biting. The whole squad always lunched together on the day after a match, usually Mondays. It's still the same today. If I'm in Madrid at the beginning of the week, I know where to find the old players who are still there: they'll be in the same place at 12.30 pm as always; I don't have to ask.

Anyway, that's one of the reasons why we were such a good team: the relationships between us were so good. I think that these days it's very difficult to do something similar at the top level of football. In Hungary today, for example, there is no shared sense of friendship and personal affection amongst current players, nothing like the feeling we had for each other at Honved. Individuals live much more separate lives now; it's a feature of modern life in general. But teams built around good players and harmonious relationships – like Honved and Real Madrid during their great periods – are very hard to beat. There was quality right through those sides. We could almost always win if we wanted to, as the records show.

I suppose the main difference in training between Real and Honved was its toughness. At Madrid, there was a very hard pre-season: short but arduous. We were very careful not to get injured during this training which involved developing real strength, running up and down a hill, followed by a lot of work with a ball. We also spent time practising how we would stay fairly close to one another during a match, so that passes need only cover a minimum of ground and could be executed with great accuracy and weight. By 1961, with five consecutive European Cup wins behind us, we had hit another 'golden' period; we kept the training as simple as we could, no surprises. By then, Miguel Munoz was coach. He had stopped playing for Real just as I arrived – he had captained the side and had been a very good player. He was a very consistent man who remained with the club for thirteen years and even coached the Spanish national team *[1968–69]*. When he had his testimonial match, that was the first time I played against Pele when São Paulo came for the occasion. Pele was just seventeen.

The money

Puskas: I didn't cost Real Madrid a penny in transfer fees. I was never bought or sold in my career. In Hungary, of course, I was officially an 'amateur' player who had deserted his club (and the army). But once I had served my FIFA ban, I was a free agent, able to go anywhere they'd have me.

The pay at Madrid was good, though not on the same planet as today, and we got bonuses for cup and league victories. When we went off to play friendlies in the close season (Real were much in demand everywhere), we had the chance to make some significant extra money. The deal was, for friendly matches, we were allowed to have a bet on winning, and that added a bit of edge to our performances after a long, hard season. We always got a cut, too, of the money the host club put up to get us there. We would get it in pesetas when we returned home, divided up equally amongst the players, usually a few days after the match. These were not contractual obligations of the club, we just talked to the cashier and it was all sorted out.

Everything was very well organised by the club. Before we set off, every player got a pack of club badges and pennants to give away. Travel arrangements were always smooth. We met up at the club before leaving and everyone received the necessary papers, passports, foreign currency and so on. There were always copies of the itinerary, hotel details and phone numbers, so that you could let your family know exactly where you would be at what time. No one ever had to ask, 'What time is the flight back?'

As for today, I suspect there's too much money in football chasing too few good players. But sometimes, the right player for a team costs a fortune but is well worth it if he brings European success and the financial prizes that go with it these days. The big clubs like to buy 'names' and the smaller ones must rely on developing the talent of the future.

Life on the pitch

Puskas: Every team in the Spanish league had a couple of players out there simply to clobber you. It wasn't too difficult to avoid the brawny ones – you could see them coming and get the hell out of it. It was the brainy ones that worried me. The Seville defender Campara was very canny and as tough as old boots, and Espanol had two young lads who thought football was the same as fighting, judging by the kicking and punching they went in for. They seemed to have been bred for the role, but at least they were predictable and didn't give me too much of a problem.

I did get sent off a few times at Real, usually for swearing at the ref because I wasn't getting the protection I thought I should be. (It was much worse when I was a youngster; then I really did have difficulty controlling myself sometimes.) Typically, the occasions I remember best are those when I was unfairly dismissed. I think the worst was one time Real played in Vienna *[European Cup quarter-final v Wiener Sport-Club, 1959]*. We were on the attack and I was going past the defender Barschandt on the right-hand touchline. He couldn't catch me and as I left him he took my legs away from behind. I went head over heels and as my feet came down, there was Barschandt's head. The Swiss referee sent me straight off. With ten men, the team played out a 0–0 draw.

Of course, I was banned for the second leg. There had been lots of publicity about the sending-off, so the club sent me with flowers to the airport with the welcoming party to receive the Austrians. We certainly gave them a good welcome later on at the Bernabeu Stadium. We stuffed them 7–1. No problem.

Friendships and rivalry with Barcelona

Puskas: The great inter-city rivalry in Spain is between Madrid and Barcelona, and the Barça football club were Real's greatest opponents (true even today). Guess who was also at Barça then? Not only Czibor and Kocsis, but also Kubala.

Laszlo Kubala's footballing life ran almost in parallel to Puskas's own, and there is a considerable resonance between them. Kubala was an exceptionally good Hungarian player who developed a complicated international career in the days when you could play consecutively for more than one national team. Born in Budpest in the same year as Puskas (1927), he played for Ferencvaros and three times for Hungary until, in 1946, his family moved to Czechoslovakia, for whom he played in eleven international matches. He returned to Hungary and signed for Vasas in 1950, winning three more Hungarian caps before defecting to Spain while on a representative tour in the same year. Despite the vehement objections of the Hungarian FA, the Spanish accepted his registration and in 1951 Kubala joined Barcelona, winning four league titles and five cup medals in his illustrious career with the club. He won more international caps, playing nineteen times for Spain before finally becoming Spain's national manager in 1969.

Puskas: All three of the Hungarians were already established at Barcelona before I arrived at Madrid. While we were winning the European Cups in 1959 and 1960, Barça were winning the league twice on the run. They had a great team then and seemed to be able to 'do' us any time they wanted. The Hungarian lads there took the piss mercilessly, of course, during this period, even phoning me up to rub it in. We were runners-up in both of Barça's championship seasons; the second time was only decided on goals scored.

But revenge is sweet. We won five championships on the trot after that, and the boot was on the other foot. My turn to make the phone calls. They couldn't seem to get hold of the ball against us, especially at the Bernabeu. When I played in Barcelona we would always rendezvous after the match in either Czibor's or Kocsis's apartment; but in Madrid I never saw them after the game.

The death of Kocsis

Puskas: Kocsis played on at Barça until 1966, I think; Czibor left earlier. Kocsis had some great years there and came to love the club deeply. They certainly were a good side. I met Kocsis for the last time in the mid-seventies, at a charity match at

Offenbach, Germany. Di Stefano was there, so were Uwe Seeler, Bobby Charlton and others. Czibor had come from Barcelona, bringing Kocsis with him, though he was already having problems with his legs and couldn't play. Czibor took him to a famous German orthopaedic surgeon in the town and had some special shoes made for him.

Kocsis remained in Barcelona after his retirement, running a cafe and playing another game he enjoyed greatly: chess. His physical problems started in 1974 with an accident at his home in Spain, when a small cupboard fell on to his foot. Kocsis did not seek any medical advice even though the foot didn't heal, and by the time he did see a doctor, the foot had to be amputated. At around the same time, a cancer was located in his stomach and he underwent a series of operations. Kocsis became very depressed after these operations and started drinking heavily. He returned to Budapest for the first time in 1976, and again three years later. He died in Barcelona – almost certainly of his own volition – in July 1979.

Puskas: It was very sad what happened to Kocsis at the end. It was in the late 1970s that he got very ill. It was cancer. An operation followed and he recovered a little for a while. I remember he had to keep to a very strict diet, and he returned to Hungary for more examinations. I don't think the doctors told him just how serious it was and he became very ill again, getting hospitalized in Budapest, then in Barcelona. He was in great pain, I believe, and when someone left a window open near to his bed, despite hardly being able to move, he managed to throw himself out of the window and finish it. Who can blame him? He was only fifty-one years old.

Vandor: I went to see Kocsis in hospital in Budapest. I think I was the last person to interview him. He was very depressed. As I was leaving, he asked me to shut the door on my way out. It disturbed me, and I asked an attendant to keep the door open and keep an eye on him. He didn't kill himself then, but later – in the Barcelona hospital – someone must have shut the door and given him the chance to end his life.

Puskas: I have enormous respect for his memory. He was a truly great striker, with a record that speaks for itself. There was a certain strangeness about him and he could be very withdrawn in company he didn't know well, but, after a difficult start, I got on very well with him over the years.

The 1960 European Cup Final: Real Madrid 7 Eintracht Frankfurt 3

On 18 May 1960, the city of Glasgow played host to one of the most famous and celebrated club matches in football's history. It was Real Madrid's fifth consecutive European Cup Final, but for Puskas it was his first. The match was watched by a huge, largely Scots crowd at Hampden Park, and broadcast 'live' on BBC television to a Europe-wide audience.

Puskas: Despite the scoreline, that match in Glasgow was a very tough game against an Eintracht team that had beaten some good sides *[including Glasgow Rangers, 6–1 and 6–3 in the semi-finals]* and whom we didn't know very well. There were 135,000 fans in Hampden Park that evening and it was one of those blissful times when the whole team seemed to play brilliantly and we almost achieved some kind of footballing perfection.

Del Sol had arrived at Madrid earlier that year and he was fantastic that night. Although considerably smaller, he was a 'Duncan Edwards' for us: great natural skill, never stopped running, superb strength on the ball. He was a little tiger. Alfredo, of course, was brilliant too.

In the run-up to that match, we played our normal league game on the Sunday and left for Glasgow the following day. I already knew Hampden from my days with Hungary. It was a huge place with a good playing surface, though perhaps not as perfect as Wembley. But hardly anyone in the club knew much about Eintracht. We were warned that they were a good side and we knew the Germans would be strong, if nothing else.

They got off to a better start than us anyway, and they were one-up before we had even opened our eyes. It was Di Stefano amongst us who woke up first and he scored two, one after the other. I hit four goals (one a penalty) on the trot after that, three in the second half, and Alfredo finished it off with his third. At 6–1, we had a bit of a rest and they got two goals, but we never cared. Everything we did seemed to come off and though we started slowly, once we hit that peak we felt we could beat any side in the world. What can I say? The whole team struck gold at the same time; it was a privilege to be there.

The Hampden crowd certainly thought so. For those present, it was an unforgettable occasion to witness, by general consent the greatest club performance of all time, rivalled only perhaps by AC Milan's stunning 4–0 victory over Barcelona thirty-four years later, in the 1994 European Cup Final. After the Glasgow match, around 40,000 Scots supporters remained on the terraces for nearly an hour simply to pay homage to the display of attacking football they had witnessed. One journalist wrote:

'The Scottish crowd knew they had seen one of the greatest ever games of club football; the only tinge of regret was that there was little hope of seeing its like again. They noted the day, 18 May 1960, and marked it as others had done Crispin's Day and counted themselves lucky to have been there.' (Widdows, 1973, p.72)

Puskas: We couldn't hear the whistle at the end for the 'Hampden Roar' all around us. Scottish fans came running on to the pitch in sheer delight. Scots players I had played against came to congratulate me after the match, and the joy at Real and in Madrid was overflowing. We were lauded by the world's media

– for a few days at least – and life was perfect. It was a wonderful match.

The journey home was incredible, but at first we couldn't get away from Glasgow. It took us a day to leave. We were paraded through the centre of town and then on to the town hall. Everywhere, cheering crowds greeted us; you'd have thought that we were *their* team that had won. Even at the airport, there were more Scots fans to see us off. Those folks certainly appreciated football.

It's strange how important playing in Britain has been in my life. That Real game in 1960 and the 6–3 at Wembley with Hungary were fantastic matches to have been involved in; to be at the very heart of football's history, not once but *twice*. But I'll tell you, it wasn't easy to go out for that game in Glasgow. I was thirty-three years old. I had a bad feeling in the pit of my stomach in the dressing-room beforehand. I was thinking, 'You're not twenty any more, are you up to this?'

But almost like magic, once I stepped out on to that grass, it all washed away. It's been true all my life; despite all the pre-match fears, when I reach the pitch I feel, 'I can do this. I know how to do it and I want to do it.' That's how I was able to play to a footballer's old age. I had to take care of myself, of course, and sometimes I didn't play as well as I wanted to. But in my life I never felt that I would get beaten. Whether it be with Honved, Hungary or Real Madrid, I've always felt, 'We can't lose' – like a gift of confidence and I don't know why. If we did lose, I always thought it was our own fault; we lost concentration or something.

The match ball

Puskas: In Glasgow, I got four goals, Di Stefano three, and the German, Stein, scored twice. As the last moments of the match approached, Alfredo and I were playing 'keep-ball', passing the ball back and forward to one another. We sometimes did this at the end of a match that we knew we'd won. It was a little game we played between us to see who could grab the ball at the end. It was always handy to have match balls for the many requests we got from fans and organizations. On this occasion, I had glanced at the ref's watch and I was counting the last minute in my mind to make sure the ball was at *my* feet when he blew the whistle. I'd scored the most, so I figured if the ball was anyone's, it was mine. But I knew Alfredo had hit a hat-trick and would grab it if he could. As the whistle blew, the ball was with me. I picked it up and was walking towards the centre-circle, when Stein came over and asked for it. At first I wasn't having any of it, but after the third time he asked me, I thought, 'I really want this ball, but this guy's scored two and lost the match. It's the least I can do.' So I gave it to him. Presumably the 1960 match ball is still with him in Germany.

World champions

Sebes: 'I was in Italy for the 1960 summer Olympic Games when a Spanish official asked me to come back with him to Madrid to watch the Intercontinental Cup match between Real Madrid and Penarol. He knew that I would be very curious to see how Puskas was playing – I hadn't seen him play for three years – but I explained that I needed a visa and permission from the Hungarian authorities. The next day, he arrived with air tickets, an official invitation and everything; the visa from the Spanish Embassy was no problem and I got the permission from Budapest to go.'

Puskas: After the Glasgow match, we played the South American champions, Penarol from Uruguay, in the first World Club Championship. In the first leg away, tactically we just looked for a draw, making certain we didn't lose. Back at home in the Bernabeu, we gave them a 5–1 hammering. Having played them once, we'd worked them out. We were three-nil up within ten minutes, but we kept it going, almost non-stop attack. Our fans were ecstatic, getting the chance to celebrate the whole season in one go, and there was a fantastic atmosphere in the stadium that night and an unbelievable party afterwards. Even during the match, with a capacity crowd inside, thousands were gathered outside just to be close to it. We were the best club in the world.

Sebes: 'It was a wonderful match, played in front of about 125,000 in the Bernabeu Stadium. Puskas was brilliant, scoring two and making two more. After the match, he invited me back to his house to celebrate Aniko's eighth birthday and we had a great time, though I noticed that Puskas only opened the bottle of champagne and said, 'Cheers'. He didn't drink any of it. It was our first chance to talk for ages; he asked about how things were in Budapest, and we talked too of old times. When he spoke, I realized how difficult those early days had been in Madrid, especially the battles with Carniglia. But by now, he was as popular in the Spanish capital as ever he'd been at his height in Budapest. I mean, in the mornings, there were taxis literally queuing up in front of his house for the privilege of taking him in for training. If the traffic lights were red on his way, police would stop the moving cars to wave him through. It was great to see him. He had tears in his eyes as we parted at the airport.'

Next season (1960–61)

Puskas: After the heights come the depths. Next season in the European Cup we got knocked out in the second round by, worst of all, Barcelona. That's football. You have to do it all again straight away.

The first leg in Madrid was a 2–2 draw and we lost the second leg 2–1. Both matches were a bit weird. The referee in Madrid had a good reputation but he really took it easy on them; you could almost say he scored for them. It was another Englishman of course, Arthur Ellis I think, and he gave a heavily disputed penalty when Kocsis was brought down on a run just outside the box. My one-time Hungarian striking partner did his famous forward-roll into the penalty area and the ref blew for the spot-kick. The linesman's flag had gone up (we thought for offside).

Ellis: 'In the last minute of this all-Spanish first leg, Kocsis was brought down by a Real Madrid version of a rugby tackle and I awarded a penalty from which Barcelona scored. The Real players, who had been leading 2–1, attempted to have the award changed. I gathered that it was "accidental". Some accident!' (Ellis, 1962, p.94)

Puskas: There was no point arguing (though that didn't stop some of us). I didn't say anything to Kocsis before the second leg, but I could see that he didn't want to meet my eyes. In the match in the Nou Camp, we had *three* goals disallowed (another English ref too, Reg Leafe). I was so mad with that ref.

Barcelona went on to reach the European Cup Final that season where they met Benfica in the Wankdorf Stadium, Berne, the very same ground where the Hungarians had lost the World Cup Final in 1954. For Czibor and Kocsis, it was the return of a nightmare. In a gripping game, Barça went ahead first; lost two quick goals, and went 3–1 down in the second half; Czibor got one back with 15 minutes to go but, despite desperate attempts to equalize, Barça lost the match 3–2.

Puskas: Czibor and Kocsis wept bitter tears on that same ground where the Golden Squad had lost the only match we dropped in a six-year run. I didn't see the games, but I heard afterwards how hard they took the defeat. They were on a huge bonus for a win as well; perhaps that brought added tears to their eyes.

As Spanish champions, Real Madrid were in the European Cup the following season, where they met the Budapest club Vasas in the opening round. Puskas was not allowed by the club to risk a return to Hungary.

Puskas: Bernabeu said to me, 'You're not playing. I don't want any problems.' It was clear he meant political problems. He told me to rest for a week. If he'd have asked me to play, I'd have said yes. I always wanted to play football. But I think he was wise, looking back at it now.

In the quarter-final, Real met Juventus and beat them 1–0 in Turin but lost – for the first time at home in Europe – by the same score in the second leg. The third game was played in Paris and Real won 3–1.

Puskas: John Charles was playing for Juve. He was a giant with legs like an elephant, enormously strong. Our defender Santamaria had been having a right old tussle with him. After the match, I had to intervene at one point to calm things down as there was a war of words developing. I told our boys, 'Keep quiet, the match is over; what's the point of arguing about it now?' It was hilarious, really: half the argument conducted in Spanish, the other half in English. Neither could really appreciate the other's insults.

We were expecting a hard match after the two earlier games and our defence was determined to be strong. This was the decider – a big game between two giant clubs who both desperately wanted to win at almost any price. John Charles towered over Santamaria and was broader across the shoulders too, so our man was reduced to kicking him. Mind you, he got a few back as well, I remember.

Another European Cup Final, another hat-trick
Benfica 5 Real Madrid 3

In the Olympic Stadium in Amsterdam in 1962, Real met the reigning champions Benfica, coached by Puskas's old adversary Bela Guttmann. At half-time Real led 3–2, thanks to Puskas's second hat-trick in a European Cup Final. But vital parts of the Real team were getting old – principally Puskas and Di Stefano – and the second half saw Coluna equalize and a young man called Eusebio score twice to win it for Benfica. At the end of the match, Puskas gave his shirt to the youngster and many of those watching saw the gesture as symbolic: a 'passing of the baton' from one of Europe's greatest, enduring – but ageing – stars to the new talent arriving on the scene.

Puskas: It was another match where the refereeing was crucial. This time it wasn't an Englishman in charge: it was Leo Horn, the Dutchman who'd refereed the 6–3 game at Wembley. Di Stefano was repeatedly fouled in the penalty area without getting anything, and they got a very dodgy penalty in the second half. (I told Mr Horn after the match that we could positively feel his friendship with Guttmann during the game.) We had scored thirty goals in four rounds plus the final; I had got a hat-trick, of course, and still ended up on the losing side. The three joint top scorers in Europe that year were all from Real: myself, Alfredo and Tejada, with seven apiece.

After the game, Eusebio came over to me and asked for my shirt. I gave it to him, why not? He was already looking a very good player with wonderful skills, and he went on to become a good friend, too. I just gave him my shirt as a gesture of friendship; never thought any more about it than that.

At Real, the mood was gloomy. Everyone was deeply upset about the refereeing of the match, and I couldn't help remembering the disallowed 'second' goal at Wembley in 1953 which Leo Horn has since admitted was a perfectly good one.

But that's football. For Real it was a bitter fruit to suck on. We knew we had played well, felt in control of the match, but lost in the end. No club can win all the time.

Another World Cup, another country

Puskas was to make one last showing at the World Cup Finals. In 1962, both he and Di Stefano were in the Spanish squad in Chile, though Di Stefano's injury did not allow him to play. In Real Madrid, Spain may have possessed the greatest club team in the world, but they did not do well in the World Cup, coming bottom of their group with only one win (over Mexico, 1–0).

Puskas: When I first signed the contract with Real, I was virtually a Spanish citizen within two days. I do remember travelling on that first tour to Argentina using my Hungarian passport, but by the time I returned, there was a Spanish one waiting for me. That meant I was available for the Spanish national team because this was before FIFA changed their ruling to exclude anyone who had already played for another country. I played in four matches for Spain, scoring two goals.

The biggest match for the Spanish team in Chile was against world champions Brazil, in Vina del Mar. Pele wasn't fit and Brazil needed a victory to stay in the competition. Spain's manager Herrera dropped Suarez, Santamaria and Del Sol, and Puskas played for the injured Di Stefano. He had a good match too, but five minutes from time Pele's stand-in, Amarildo, scored the winner in a 2–1 victory.

Puskas: It wasn't easy to play for another national team and I don't think many players managed it very well. You were already fleeing from somewhere and that brought all its own problems with it. I was glad to serve in the Spanish team. Spain had given me that second chance that I needed so badly; I had succeeded since arriving and was very grateful for everything. I felt I owed the Spanish people my best, and that's what they got.

Real Madrid on the wane

It looked like the writing was on the wall for the great Real side, though at home they kept on winning the league title. In the 1962–63 season they went out of the European Cup to Anderlecht in the first round, conceding three goals in a draw at the Bernabeu and losing 1–0 in Holland. Like the old Hungarian team, the Real defence had often leaked goals in the past, but with their football so dedicated to attack it usually didn't matter, as Di Stefano, Puskas et al always scored more at the other end. But both players were now thirty-six years old, and the goals weren't coming like they used to.

Spanish champions yet again in 1963, Real entered the European Cup for the eighth consecutive year in the autumn. Glasgow Rangers were on the end of a 6–0 hiding in Madrid in the first round (another Puskas hat-trick); Real scored eight goals against Dynamo Bucharest over the two legs of the second round; they beat AC Milan 4–0 in the Bernabeu to ensure a semi-final place against FC Zurich, and they put eight past the Swiss side over two legs to reach yet another European Cup Final, this time against the ultra-defensive Internazionale, coached by Helenio Herrera, in the Prater Stadium, Vienna. Amongst the Inter team was one Mazzola 'junior'. Puskas's professional career now spanned over two decades and he found himself competing against the sons of players he had faced in the past.

Real lost the match 3–1, with young Mazzola getting two of Inter's goals. For Di Stefano, blamed by some for 'selfishness', by others for being too slow, it was the end of the European line. The two-times winner of the European Player of the Year award didn't appear again to grace the competition in which he had played such a tremendous early role.

Puskas: When a team loses a match, there's always a media search for a scapegoat. I don't think our loss was Di Stefano's fault. He played well nine times out of ten and it isn't fair to blame him. He always made a terrific effort but sometimes he was more successful than others. I think Inter played better than us on the day and were worthy winners. I didn't like the kind of football they played, with everyone behind the ball (a system which the Swiss adopted first in the 1940s), which unfortunately is the way the current Hungarian side play too. The drift of football towards massive concentration on defence and hoping for quick breakaway goals hastened the end of my career. It wasn't much fun any more.

The bulk of my playing career was about getting goals – as many as possible. For Real in Europe, I got 35 in 37 matches, including four in one final and three in another. I always tried to take up positions where I could be seventy-five per cent sure that the ball would reach me. If a chance came, I took it without hesitation and I usually got it on target, but I think I made a lot of goals too.

Testimonial match

Puskas was still at Real Madrid two years later when the club reached yet another European Cup Final in 1966. He didn't play in that match, which saw Real reclaim the title with a 2–1 win over Partizan Belgrade, but he took part in the early rounds. For his European finale, he knocked in four goals against Feyenoord at home in the first round. The second round was at Kilmarnock, on 17 November 1965. Puskas says he remembers nothing of this, his last European game – a 2–2 draw – but of course, at the time, he would not have known it would be his final appearance in the competition. In Madrid, he was increasingly overseeing the emergence of young players like Valasquez and Amancio, realizing that his playing career was very near its close. But there was one great, emotional night ahead at the Bernabeu Stadium for Puskas: the evening when nearly

80,000 Real fans paid their respects to one of the greatest players ever to have worn the all-white strip of their star-spangled club.

Puskas: I was very proud to have played at the top to the ripe old age of forty, especially when I recalled that many had written me off a decade before. But playing all those years had taken it out of me and I was deeply tired. I left Madrid in 1967, but returned two years later for a testimonial match in the Bernabeu Stadium on 26 May 1969. It was a great gift from the club – I could keep all the receipts except for the expenses of the incoming team – and it was something the club normally offered only to those who had served ten years there. I had played for nine years, but the chairman allowed both me and Santamaria to be exceptions. Bernabeu had offered me the testimonial not long after I finished playing. He lived quite close to me in Madrid and I often saw him out walking with his wife. We would stop for a chat; I've always enjoyed his company and his sense of humour. Anyway, I told him I didn't have time for the testimonial immediately, but I would let him know when it was possible.

When the time came, it was a wonderful night. Huge numbers of supporters turned out for the occasion – a Monday evening – for the match against Rapid Vienna. I appeared only for twenty minutes or so, got some nice passes, and was allowed to do a few dribbles. It was a very emotional occasion. My thoughts wandered back to those barefoot kids in Kispest, and especially to my friend Bozsik, wishing he could have been there for the occasion. Two days later, in the same stadium on the Wednesday night, the European Cup Final between Ajax and AC Milan was played and only 30,000 turned out to watch it. When I think that nearly 80,000 had come to my testimonial two nights earlier, it amazes me. There was a huge reception afterwards, with many gifts graciously presented to me. They had learned to love me in the end.

12

Retirement and Coaching, 1967–91

'I often sat in a wicker armchair on the touchline with a ball at my feet.'

After his appearances for Spain in the 1962 World Cup in Chile, Puskas effectively retired from playing at international level. Meanwhile, Hungarian football had picked itself up and the system of coaching and organization laid down in the days when Sebes was in charge began once again to produce high-quality players in considerable numbers. Prominent amongst them were Florian Albert and Ferenc Bene. Hungary had reached the quarter-finals in Chile and did so again four years later in England. Puskas was at Goodison Park to see them.

Puskas: In 1966, I went to Liverpool to watch Hungary play Brazil at Everton's ground. We beat the world champions 3–1, but Pele didn't play because of injury and Brazil were not a good side. The Hungarian team was quite good – Florian Albert and Bene stood out – but not good enough. I watched the Soviet

Union beat them 2–1 in the quarter-final at Roker Park, and followed a few of the England games including the Final. It was a good match, though I think one of the English goals was disputed, wasn't it?

Puskas ran into a number of old colleagues in England, including Lajos Tichy.

Tichy: I was getting on a bit by 1966, and I hadn't originally been chosen for the Hungarian World Cup squad but I had a good season and got included just before we left. By then, all the formal suits had already been made for the players. I was given the suit made for a guy about two metres tall (who got left out) and it drowned me. When I met Puskas in England, he was at the airport to greet us. The first thing he said to me was: 'Who's your tailor?' That was typical of his sense of humour.

Puskas: I think it's very difficult to judge a team by what happens in World Cup games. The matches seem out of the usual rhythm. The most difficult games of all are the qualifiers and the latter stages of the finals. There is enormous pressure and, on the world stage, players want to do something great that will be remembered for ever, and it rarely comes off. How many World Cup games have been really worth watching? And the Final is often awful (though England v West Germany was an exception). When players get that far, everyone is exhausted and terrified. The weight of responsibility and the desire for success are too heavy to bear. The players just want to win and get the hell out of there. They can rarely play their natural game under these pressures. Take Hungary in 1966, for example. They played well against Brazil, but the real pressure game was against the Soviet Union for a place in the semi-final. In that match, the Hungarians didn't seem to be able to hit simple passes to one another, never mind anything else. And look at ourselves in 1954: unbeatable for six years – except for one match, and that happened to be the World Cup Final – but who were the real champions?

Another trip to Liverpool

Puskas: 1966 was not my first time in Liverpool. I always liked the working-class cities of England; the rows of terraced houses and the absence of skyscrapers. It all seemed on a very human scale. But Liverpool is a special place, both for its football teams and facilities and also for the great river views from the hill near Everton *[Everton Brow]* with those huge docks all along the bank. I didn't see much of the local teams playing because in those days the matches weren't on TV. Later on in my life, I often visited England to stay with a very good friend there who has now returned, like me, to Budapest. In England, he would drive me round to watch matches, especially in Manchester and Liverpool.

Over the following decade and more, Puskas would play in unnumbered 'friendly' 'Old Boy' and 'charity' matches. He was often more than willing to lend his name and prestige without any financial reward for himself. One trip to Liverpool in early May 1967 demonstrates the spontaneous generosity Puskas could produce on occasions. He turned out, free of charge, at Holly Park, South Liverpool's little football ground, in a fund-raising match for a small community centre in Garston. Brian Taylor was responsible for the coup of bringing him there.

Taylor: To tell the truth, it was all done a little tongue-in-cheek. I'd run a charity match the year before, during the World Cup, so this year I decided to go for one of the very top players in the world: Puskas. Why not? So I wrote to Real Madrid, with a letter asking if he might play in our fund-raising match. Amazingly, we soon received a telegram from Puskas himself, which read: 'Received your letter of 7th. I only wait you send me plane ticket. Puskas.' We framed that telegram and it's still in my office today.

I went down to London to meet him with the Spanish Consulate from Liverpool. (This guy had told me I was crazy trying to get Puskas for this match.) Meeting Puskas off the plane from Madrid, we went for lunch accompanied by an Iberian Airline hostess who had been kindly loaned to us to interpret and help break the ice while we waited for the connecting flight to Liverpool. Puskas was quite portly in appearance, shorter than I expected too. He weaved a web of charm over this delightful hostess during the lunch, chatting her up in Spanish. He succeeded in getting her telephone number, that's for sure.

At Speke airport, we were astounded by the reception waiting for us. All the other passengers were asked to get off the plane first and, when we descended, there was this amazing battery of cameras flashing and reporters calling out. The Dunlop Tyre Company provided a chauffeur-driven car for the duration of his stay and he was whisked off to the Adelphi Hotel.

He did everything we asked of him and wanted nothing in return, which says a lot about the character and stature of the man. He was an enormously friendly, outgoing person, pumping hands wherever he went, saying 'Puskas,' to people he met, as if he needed any introduction. A Spanish priest turned up and showed him round a bit; took him, I think, to a Spanish waiters' club.

The night before the match, he mentioned to me how he wished he'd brought some small souvenirs from Real Madrid to give to people. At 6 pm the next day, as he got out of his car at the ground, he handed me a parcel of badges and pennants. He had phoned Madrid in the morning and asked the club officials to send a parcel by plane to London, have it transferred to a flight to Liverpool and driven by taxi to his hotel. I guess that's what you call 'clout'. I mean, this guy had already retired, he wasn't a current player who they needed to keep sweet.

We pulled John Charles over for that match; Malcolm Allison, Billy Liddell, Billy Bingham, Jimmy McIlroy, Dave Hickson. Bill Perry played too, who had scored the winner in the 1953 'Stanley Matthews' Cup Final. On the night, there were more people locked out of South Liverpool's ground than we had inside. Puskas wasn't too mobile, but he had a fantastic shot – I'd never seen power like that before – and he could bend a ball like the Brazilians. I think we raised over one thousand pounds as a result of the match – a huge sum of money for a small youth club in those days. Next year I tried to get Di Stefano!

Jim Baxter

Puskas had a reputation as someone who liked to enjoy himself wherever he went. The great Scottish player Jim Baxter – himself renowned for a brilliant career on the pitch and a fairly wild one off it – met Puskas on a number of occasions in the 1960s.

Baxter: Puskas was a bit fond of the 'jiggy-jig' and the whisky at the time, like myself. We ended up together at a party in London once. Puskas came over: 'Jimmy, Denis *[Law]*', he said, 'jiggy-jig, vhisky?' That was his English vocabulary as far as I was concerned. On another occasion, at a hotel before a testimonial match, it was the same again: 'Aye, Jimmy, jiggy-jig?' And I says, 'Well, let's get the game over first, Puski!'

Oh, he loved his whisky, Puskas, and his jiggy-jig. I remember the night Real Madrid beat us at Ibrox, one-nothing *[a first-leg European Cup match against Rangers in September 1963]*. Puskas was at the banquet after the game. He was at me again and I said wait till the banquet's finished and I'll take you to a party. Now, at that time Puskas would be possibly the best footballer in the world. I took him to the George Hotel – that was our 'headquarters' at the time, that's what we used to call it, 'our headquarters', Crerand, McKinnon and the boys – but we ended up at a house in Drumchapel, on the outskirts of Glasgow. A very, very well-known place. There's Puskas in the scullery of this Drumchapel flat jiggy-jigging, and me and McKinnon in the doorway watching him. 'There's the greatest player in the world,' I says to McKinnon, 'cop for that, there!' If you think of the stories nowadays making the paper, and there was the greatest footballer in the world in a scullery in Drumchapel, having his 'nooky'.

Puskas: I ran into Jim Baxter in Glasgow but I can't remember when. He was some guy, and we had a few strange adventures together. He was always messing about, having a laugh. I remember him dragging me off to some party or another. He was a very good player too, but I could hardly understand a word he said. I needed someone to translate him into English.

Favourite players

Puskas: In my life I have seen many very good players, too many to name individually. When I think of some of those guys I saw in the old days, playing for Czechoslovakia, Yugoslavia and the Soviet Union, I remember how much I admired their excellent technique. When I was playing for Hungary, the opposition players that stuck out were people like Walter and Rahn for Germany; Kopa and Ben Tifour for France; Ocwirk and Happel for Austria; Wright, Finney and Matthews for England; Boniperti, Capello and Meazza in Italy; Djalma Santos and Didi for Brazil; Santamaria and Schiaffino for Uruguay.

Di Stefano, of course, ranks with the greatest for me. Pele too, and of the English, Bobby Charlton was their best. I thought Denis Law was a wonderful player at Manchester, but as for George Best, I think it's difficult to include him in the very highest group because his career at the top level was too short and without real international experience.

I have been fortunate to know personally many of the world's greatest players, and I know too how much of a role 'lady luck' plays in a footballer's life. Some great players are not recognized by the world's press. For me, Bozsik was deeply under-rated. I knew his game intimately – as well as I knew my own – and I have never seen his equal on the world stage. He did things no one else could do; when he released the ball, ninety-nine times out of a hundred, not only was the pass accurate, it also went to the best possible area of the pitch. It was uncanny. I don't want to hurt anyone, but in my opinion, Bozsik was the greatest player I ever saw or knew.

Leaving Madrid, the sausage factory and the restaurant

Puskas: The prospect of retirement didn't cause me great heartache. I felt ready to stop playing. I knew I wanted to stay in football and towards the end of my playing career I began attending a coaching college, which I continued at even while doing my first coaching job, which was with a Spanish second division team called Vitoria. I started there within a couple of weeks of retiring as a player and stayed for sixteen months, but towards the end of my contract I began to heartily dislike the place.

I also had some business interests in Spain. At one time, while still a player, I had a sausage factory in Madrid, making 'Debrecen-style' spicy Hungarian sausages.* A friend had persuaded me to start the business and it ran for about four years, but it wasn't a good idea and I had to give it up in the end. Every morning I was off to market to buy the best meat and, what with trying to help run the place as well, it took up too much time and energy. Soon some of the crowd were getting on

* Debrecen is a city in eastern Hungary famous for its sausages.

my back because I wasn't playing very well. I had about thirty employees and, amazingly, one of them was old 'uncle' Jozsef, the local butcher from Kispest who had once offered us a big sausage as the first football prize we ever played for. But the Spanish currency was always losing value through inflation and it wasn't worth the hassle in the end.

I opened a restaurant too, a beautiful place about a hundred metres away from the Bernabeu Stadium. I really loved the place; it was fantastic. I thought it was one of the best in Spain. All kinds of celebrities came to eat there; actors, artists, movie stars, footballers, the lot. I had a brilliant cook (and I've always loved cooking myself) and there was a range of dishes: French, Spanish, Hungarian. There was a room upstairs for about a hundred and twenty guests – white linen on all the tables – and a bar in the basement which was bursting at the seams every night. God, I loved that place! Why did I ever let it go?

I'll tell you why, some fools persuaded me to go to Vancouver, that's why. Some Hungarians who lived in Canada, and also an American businessman I'd met, talked me into it, telling me that 'soccer' was about to take off in North America, and like an idiot, I went. I had to sell the restaurant because my wife wasn't going to stay in Madrid and run the place alone, and my daughter was too young to take it over. The pass came; I went after the ball again – I did want to be a coach – and was left with nothing but a lovely memory.

In North America

On 25 May 1967, only a few weeks after the charity match in Liverpool, Puskas is reported in the New York Herald Tribune *(under a heading, 'Puskas, Big Fink and Kuk') as having been hired as coach of the Golden Gate Gales in the USA. The report – which also incorrectly describes Puskas as 'coach' of the famous Real Madrid team – proved unfounded. But he did go to Canada.*

Puskas: The Vancouver team I coached were the only Canadians included in the new North American professional league.* I went out there a few months before their season started and got together a collection of players, mostly Europeans – a few Spaniards, Hungarians and so on. We didn't do too badly, usually lying fourth or fifth in the sixteen-team league. I didn't have enough good players to do any better. There were quite a few South American players – principally from Uruguay and Argentina, I think – in the American teams, and one very skilful Japanese lad who stuck out called Chan Chio Ai. There were very few American players around then.

It was a strange routine, with enormous amounts of travelling involved. We would go to the USA and stay for perhaps a week, during which time we would play maybe three matches; then return to Vancouver for another three at home. Sometimes we had good crowds; sometimes not so good. There were some unbelievable downpours during matches, I remember.

My team wasn't bad, but nothing special. We came fifth but could easily have been in third place. Then, out of the blue, the North American league went bankrupt after only nine months.† It was dominated by a few big clubs and they announced that the costs – especially of the travelling – were not being recovered and the whole thing was closing down. I had no idea; just got a letter one day saying the league was finished.

Even today, I can't see 'soccer' taking off professionally in America. I was over there for the World Cup in 1994 and the problems remain the same. Children and youngsters

* This was presumably the North American Soccer League, 1968.

† In fact, the league survived until 1970, though Vancouver and eleven other clubs dropped out in 1969.

love the game and many people play it, but from high school on, there's nowhere to go with it. The only senior team is the national one; there's been no professional league despite a number of attempts since I was there to get one going. I wish them the very best, but you can't have a real national team without a pro league of your own. Maybe the current Major League Soccer will work. They say it's doing quite well, but the costs and the distances to travel are enormous.

Coaching Panathinaikos

Puskas: After Canada, I returned 'home' to Spain (and it was then that I had my testimonial match). But not long afterwards, in 1970, I went to Greece to work as a coach. It all happened very suddenly. There I am one day, sitting in my house in Madrid, and I get a visit from someone representing Panathinaikos. The club had just won the league title, but their current coach was moving on. They made me an offer and I went. I was there for four and a half years.

Panathinaikos was a very straightforward, uncomplicated little club – but it produced the best team in Greece at the time. The players were very different from those I was used to mixing with in Spain. They were a great deal less sophisticated: nice, honest lads who were very determined to succeed. And they had to be. The best players were mostly with Olympiakos or AEK Athens, so to beat them, we needed that bit of extra effort and commitment.

When I arrived, I tried to explain what I expected of them and attempted to give them some idea of my vision of how the game should be played. I told them if they had a go at doing it my way, I would stay and give it my best shot. I found I got on very well with these lads, and they really made an effort to keep strictly to the recommendations I was making. I also tried, with some success I think, to develop the kind of mutual friendships within the squad that good, harmonious football requires. So we would all go out regularly together to the cinema or whatever, and a good spirit was encouraged that showed itself in the success we gained.

The European Cup, 1970–71

Puskas: We had a good run in the European Cup in my first season with Panathinaikos. We beat Jeunesse Esch 2–1 away and 5–0 at home in the first round. In the quarter-finals we drew Everton, and I honestly didn't think we'd stand much of a chance against the English champions. I told the players to just relax and play; try to help one another all the time. I didn't give them any fancy tactical instructions; you can draw a lot of pictures on the board, but have you got the players to do it with? Anyway, we drew 1–1 at Goodison and held them to 0–0 at home to go through on the away goal. So it was the semis next, against one of the best teams in Europe: Red Star Belgrade.

We got murdered in Belgrade, 4–1. There wasn't much we could have done about it, frankly; the score reflected the real difference in class between the two sides. But not long after the first leg, when we had returned to Greece, one of the military chiefs who ran the country – this one was in charge of the Sports Ministry – came to me and said, 'How could you possibly lose 4–1? The government won't allow it.' I told him it was eminently possible to lose 4–1 against a good team, and suggested that perhaps he should have played centre-forward and got a couple more goals himself. I told him not to worry, there was still one more leg to go and at least we had an away goal.

Anyway, the matter didn't rest there. I was summoned to his office in Athens and told that the return leg had to be played in the Olympiakos stadium. I was getting a bit annoyed at this point, and told him *he* could play at Olympiakos's ground if he wanted but I wasn't having any of it; the match would be played where it belonged, on our own home ground. I was told it was an order, so I said, 'I'm off, then. Get someone else to do it.'

All this took about a week in various exchanges, and I was a bit disappointed that the club didn't back me up more on this. In the end, it was the players that convinced me to stay. They said, 'Maestro, don't leave us now when we are so close to such a big game,' and so on. So I relented and remained, but I didn't think we would win in that massive ground with the fans so far away from the action. I wanted it in our place because it was so intimate and intense there.

I shouldn't have worried. When the evening of the match came along, the stadium was packed so tight a flea couldn't have found room. There were fans everywhere, even dangling from places you would have thought it impossible to reach. A fantastic, frenzied atmosphere. I tried to relax the players as much as I could. I told them they had nothing to lose at this point, just go for a big win, play your game and don't worry about theirs, hit the back of the net. That's football.

They did it, too. In the second minute, there was panic in the Red Star penalty area when one of their defenders lost control of the ball. We had this huge lad Antoni Antoniadis, about six feet three inches tall with legs like tree trunks *[top scorer in the European Cup that year, with ten goals]*, and he got to it and knocked it in. At half-time it was still 1–0. The lads came in with their heads down, and I said, 'Come on, this is your chance for glory. You can win this.'

They really gave it everything in the second half. We were more or less constantly on the attack, but Red Star were a very good side and defended in depth. Fifteen minutes in, and a cross from the wing reached our giant boy for the second, with his head. The place went crazy. You could almost lean on the noise. The fans were chanting some of the weirdest stuff I've heard; you couldn't hear yourself think. There was no point me trying to pass any instructions on, it was impossible, but I brought our best midfield player *[Domazos]* a bit wider on the right, where Bozsik used to play, so he could read the game from there. With fifteen minutes to go, he hit a beauty and we were three-up and through to the final if we could keep them out until the whistle.

Everyone was shouting 'Defend, boys, defend', but I was screaming 'Attack!' If you just defend, you lose. It was incredibly tense. With two minutes to go, their right-half hit a powerful shot from a few yards out and it was brilliantly saved by our goalie *[Oeconomopoulos]*; he dived like a tiger through the air to clutch it and save the match for us. At the end, the players were ecstatic; so was the crowd. I congratulated them all – they had reached the European Cup Final, a great achievement – and then I slipped off quietly home.

I heard later that the military chief had appeared in the dressing-room after the match asking for me but he was told that I'd already gone. He called me at home but I said I was too tired to talk. He continued to call over the next few days, five or six times, and I finally agreed to meet him, if simply to have the pleasure of telling him to his face that he had given up the ghost ten days before the victory. Anyway, the players and the club officials were absolutely delighted with things and the government suddenly became very helpful. For the fans, of course, it was wonderful. A small club in the final of the greatest club competition of them all. At last their dreams had come true, but there was still one more match to play: against Ajax, who were themselves about to hit a glorious period, with a Golden Squad all of their own.

The European Cup Final

Puskas: They had a few useful players in the Ajax team, like Cruyff, Neeskens, Muhren and Van Dijk. They had been developing 'total football' for a while. They moved all over the pitch; the left-back could play right-wing. Only the most technically skilful players – and in peak physical condition too – could play this kind of game.

I knew our chances were slim, so I approached the same military man, the 'sports minister', to seek permission to strengthen my squad. I wanted to sign two players from Salonika, one a forward, the other a midfielder, whom I'd been watching for some time. The rule was that I could sign these players up to six weeks from the end of the season but I needed his permission first. These two boys were very quick and I wanted the extra pace to trouble the Dutchmen. I was quite prepared to let them play for Salonika in the league right up to the end of the season, I just wanted them for the final. He refused permission.

The Final was played at Wembley in front of a crowd of 83,000. Ajax won 2–0 but Panathinaikos were not embarrassed. Van Dijk put the Dutch club ahead after only five minutes, but they had to wait until almost the end of the match before getting their second, an own goal. Ajax, of course, went on to win the Champions Cup three times on the run.

Puskas: On the day, Ajax were better than us, but not by all that much. I think with those two quick players we might have stood a chance. At the end of the match, there was a mad scramble in our area and they kicked the goalie and the ball into the net. The (English) ref didn't seem too interested. One good thing that did come out of it for the club was the invitation to play the South American champions in the Intercontinental matches (Ajax had refused the chance). We drew at home and lost 2–1 in Uruguay, which illustrated that we were a pretty good side, just short of a couple of top-class players. Anyway, all the club's people in Athens were absolutely delighted with our progress.

We won three league titles when I was at Panathinaikos, although one was subsequently taken away. It was right at the end of the season; a big match away to Olympiakos. The winner would take the championship. We were on the attack and there was a clear penalty but it wasn't given. The ref wasn't 'with us', you see. But it was still a draw and that meant we would take the title. The atmosphere inside the ground was intense and the fans were very volatile. Right after the penalty incident there was a pitch invasion, with fans fighting each other on the field. It went completely out of control and I took my players off the pitch and went home. We were heavily criticized and the title was awarded to Olympiakos by default.

The travelling coach

Puskas: At a big match like that semi-final against Red Star, it's not the coach who really carries the burden, it's the players. The coach can try to set the mood, talk through the game, encourage and explain, but in the end it's the players who have to solve the real problems on the pitch. You also need a good team behind you: trainers, physios, a doctor, all of which were in place at Panathinaikos.

The thing about coaching, or 'managing' as the English still call it, is not so much the assessing of individual playing ability – you can see that in a day – it's much more about the development of relationships that are going to work for the team. When I arrived at a club, I liked to get away to a training camp with all the players, where there was an opportunity to talk (as much as train) and to get to know who these boys were. I think I was very lucky in my coaching career, as good relationships between myself and the players usually did develop well.

The Hungarian sports journalist Kalman Vandor saw Puskas coaching the players at Panathinaikos.

Vandor: The boys were practising free-kicks and penalties. Puskas started trying to explain something to a few of them, but when he saw that nobody was getting the hang of it, he charged on to the pitch and began to demonstrate. He was better than any of them, of course, and he just carried on placing the ball in various positions and whacking it into the net. After about ten minutes of this, I shouted, 'Let them have a go now, Ocsi!' That was his strength – and his weakness – as a coach. He could demonstrate anything with a ball, but he wasn't the greatest communicator. He never bothered with any fancy tactical talks, he just said: 'Take your chances when they come!'

Puskas: I think I was at my best on the training pitch when I didn't have to speak, I could *show* what I meant. I tried to learn as much as possible from the mistakes I saw coaches make when I was a player, and I think I was most use to younger players who were still enthusiastic to learn.

I couldn't get out there on the pitch any more, that's for sure. I could kick around in training and I really tried to show those boys everything I knew. I was happy spending a couple of hours on the training pitch. At Panathinaikos, I learnt some Greek and I tried to show the players the huge variety of ways of kicking the ball that I'd seen and learnt, but sometimes it's not easy to teach players new things, not once they're over a certain age. It was a good mixture of very skilful young players and mature, older guys with a tremendous determination to win things, something that sometimes only comes as you see your career nearing its conclusion.

But there's nothing like playing. During league matches as a coach, I often sat in a wicker armchair on the touchline with a ball at my feet, sometimes juggling it about. People laughed, but you've got to do something with the energy that runs through you while watching football.

The sports writer Rob Hughes watched Puskas at one of Panathinaikos's friendly matches:

'His thirst for public adulation is still unquenchable . . . Suddenly he is on the pitch galloping 40 yards to where an *opposing* player has collapsed. He pats the fallen player on the head, leaves the player to the medicine man, and turns to acknowledge the chants of "Puskas! Puskas!" He walks back to his chair the long way round, pausing to sell a couple of Chelsea v Real Madrid replay tickets from a huge wad concealed in his tracksuit.' (*Sunday Times*, 30 May 1971)

Puskas: The only real problems in Greece were with officials and the military guys. I did have my moments with them, I'm afraid. In fact the parting of the ways was a rather nasty business. The government was changing, I think, and anyway I found myself in this big argument with a very fat guy. I ended up giving him a swift kick between the legs and leaving the country. Back to Spain.

On the road again

Puskas: I was only in Madrid about three months before the next call game, this time from Chile. It was a friend, of course, connected with the club, Colo Colo, so off I went to coach again in 1975–76. I must say that the players there were extremely skilful. I put together a good side and we came second in the league twice on the run, only one point behind Universitas. The chairman became a good friend but there were other elements at the club that began to make difficulties for me. The secretary, for example, was too often in the dressing-room trying to tell me what to do. I told him to bugger off back to his office. At least I had no problems with the language – Spanish – and I could swear with the best of them. In the end, I told the chairman I couldn't work with all these hustlers around and I resigned before the last match of my second season there. It was back to Spain again.

It wasn't long before I was off once more. This was a comparatively short trip but to a very strange country: Saudi Arabia. It was possibly the richest nation on earth and they decided they wanted a good national team. I was invited, along with my old colleague from Real Madrid, Hector Rial, and we took a good masseur from Madrid along with us too. It was fascinating there. They organized an international tournament in Riyadh and the Saudis came third, which was about right. We also played three matches in Europe which went quite well. They wanted me to stay on but my family had had enough, and Hector's wife had got ill and they both returned to Madrid. I certainly didn't want to stay there on my own – my wife and daughter always travelled with me on these jobs – and while I was there, my mother died in Budapest *[1976]* and I was unable to get out of Saudi in time; the authorities wouldn't act quickly enough and I felt bad about that.

More coaching in Spain followed that Arabian job. I was asked to help a struggling first division team and I had a go, but there wasn't much I could do, there was no time to build anything. I remember after one match – a 4–1 defeat at home – a local journalist asked me what the solution was, and I told him: 'Buy sixteen new players.' That was it; they were relegated.

Brian Clough

Puskas: Then it was back to Greece again, would you believe? I took over at AEK Athens just before the 1978–79 season. They were the champions of Greece and in the European Cup that year. We beat Porto 6–1 at home and were hanging on desperately in Portugal, losing 4–1 in the end. But we were through to the next round, where we drew Nottingham Forest.

I went to England to cast my eye over the Forest team. They had beaten the reigning champions, Liverpool, in the first round, so I knew they were serious competition. But I had no idea how odd Brian Clough was. When I visited the stadium and introduced myself, I asked for a match-ball to take back for my boys to get the feel of. He refused point blank to give me one. I thought: Go to hell, then. He's crazy. I mean, I could just go out and buy a match ball, for God's sake. What was the point of it?

AEK lost the home leg 2–1 and were well beaten, 5–1 in the second leg.

Puskas: Despite that loss, the season at AEK went reasonably well, but a major problem arose towards the end of the season. We were top of the league with two matches to play when the chairman approached me and asked if I could bring the assistant coach much closer to the work I was doing. I was blunt: 'Do you want him to do the job?' No, no, he protested, but you know how it is . . . I could see the writing on the wall, so I said goodbye. I can't stand to stay around if there is any suggestion that I'm not wanted. They paid off the rest of my contract and I left.

The death of Bozsik

Puskas: After 1956, I didn't meet up with Bozsik until the '62 World Cup in Chile. We'd been able to keep in touch by phone and letter prior to that. We were so happy to see one another again. He was my best friend, almost from birth, so it was a very emotional moment. I didn't know whether to cry or laugh. After that we met more often, usually in Vienna. We could take our wives and rendezvous there. 'Cucu' came to Madrid, once with the Honved basketball team.

Bozsik's illustrious career in the Hungarian national team – inheriting Puskas's captaincy – continued until 1962. It had an appropriately joyous ending in front of 80,000 fans in the Nepstadion. The match against Uruguay was the occasion of

Bozsik's 100th cap and he scored a terrific goal, only his eleventh for Hungary. He briefly managed Honved (1966–67) but was clearly unsuited to the role.

Puskas and Bozsik met up on odd occasions throughout the 1960s. On one such, in May 1968 at an 'Old Boys' match, Yugoslavia v Rest of Europe in Belgrade, Puskas and Bozsik played in the same team together once again. Bozsik was appointed national team coach in 1974 but after the Hungary v Austria match in Vienna on 28 September that year, he had a heart attack and entered hospital. He took the advice of the doctors and semi-retired from football. He spent the following years pottering around in the Hungarian FA's office. A man respected by everyone in the Hungarian game, Jozsef Bozsik died after another heart-attack in 1978, aged only 52.

Puskas: The worst thing was, I didn't see him before he died, though my wife was able to come to Budapest then, and visited him in hospital. She called me afterwards and said he looked much better and they would be letting him go home the next day. But I felt a foreboding; I knew it wasn't good. He died the following morning trying to get out of bed.

I didn't go back for Bozsik's funeral because I had sworn I would never return to Hungary and I stuck to it. There was the complication that, technically, I was a 'deserter' because, of course, at Honved we were all in the army, weren't we? I was suspended as a soldier after my failure to return, but the army never took any more drastic action than that. While I was at Real Madrid though, the club wouldn't have let me return anyway (even when Real drew the Hungarian club Vasas in 1961). And in those days, I didn't want to risk anything I had going for me in Spain either. I knew I could do well and look after my family there OK. But in 1978, I could have come home; there were no restrictions for me and I wasn't afraid of what might happen. It was my decision alone. It took longer for me to change my mind.

In Egypt

Puskas: The next place I went to was Egypt. I went straight there from Greece in the summer of 1979. The chairman of an Egyptian club, El Masry, was on holiday in Athens with his family. They came to visit me and Erzebet at our house, and he made a proposal that I should become his team coach. My wife was very keen. She said, 'We've never been there before; come on, let's go.' In the end I was there for five years, in Port Said. My wife soon regretted her enthusiasm but she didn't dare make anything of it. There was a point when I fell out with the club and left for Spain but, after a couple of months, they came over to persuade me to go back.

I had some ferocious arguments with the chairman, mostly over why we hadn't won the championship. The problem was that the two clubs who always ended up above us – Zamalek and Internazional – were the teams supported by the army and the state police. It was a bit like Honved and MTK in the old days in Hungary. We weren't going to be allowed to beat these two clubs in Egypt. I remember once, when we were leading the table right at the end of the season, going one goal up in a match only to have two completely ludicrous goals given against us. If we had won the game, we would have won the league. It wasn't going to happen, but this chairman couldn't see it.

Port Said was a very strange place. Dozens of ships arrived and departed every day and it was a restricted area. There were lots of shops to buy goods very cheap, but you couldn't get them out of there. When friends from Hungary visited, of course they were dying to take some stuff home with them. I could then have a chat with some of the customs people and sort something out for them. It wasn't the first time I'd done that!

There was one other Hungarian coach in Egypt at the same time as me. It was Hidegkuti.

After his return to Budapest in 1956, Hidegkuti didn't meet up with

Puskas again until 1964, when Real Madrid played Internazionale in the European Cup Final in Vienna, and he and Buzanszky went to watch the match. These old colleagues from the Golden Squad occasionally ran into one another at international occasions in subsequent years, but Egypt was the first opportunity Hidegkuti and Puskas had had to spend any regular time together since the Uprising nearly twenty years before.

Hidegkuti: I was coach at Fiorentina for a few years and then went to Egypt in 1973 for seven years. Towards the end of my stay, I had the chance to meet Puskas again. I was with a club called Nacional; he was coaching El Masry. They were quite low down the table when Puskas arrived, but they finished third. Our teams played one another four times and I won two of them.

I was based in Cairo, about 200 kilometres from Port Said, but we visited each other quite regularly. We would go out for a meal sometimes, or our wives would cook up a great Hungarian dinner at home, and we would talk of old times and current problems. Puskas got on very well with the Egyptian players. He was a strict coach but they loved him none the less. So did the Hungarian sailors who sometimes arrived on the ships in Port Said and dragged us out for endless meals.

Hidegkuti had considerable success during his time in Egypt, winning the league title five times and the cup once. He returned to Hungary in 1980 and retired but was persuaded to return to coaching in Dubai, 1985–87. Back in Hungary since then, Hidegkuti has been an 'official observer' for the FA, watching particular players every week, but recently (1996) was persuaded to return to Egypt once again on a one-year contract as technical adviser to Alexandria.

Puskas: I enjoyed my time in Egypt but it wasn't the end of my travels by any means. I did two stints in Paraguay towards the end of the 1986 and '87 seasons, only for about four months at a time, to help a friend there during the play-off stages of the league competition. Once again, as in Chile, I found the players enormously talented, particularly in ball-control techniques. I always overcame any language problems during this itinerant coaching life. Spanish is great, of course, for most of South America. I knew some English, learnt some Greek, and had a Spanish interpreter while I was working in Arabia. In Egypt, depending on which player, I needed to use Spanish, English and sometimes even Greek. My Hungarian wasn't much use to me.

I ended up in Australia, from 1988 onwards. I went to south Melbourne, the Hellas Club. A friend invited me over. At first I went without my wife, played in some 'Old Boy' matches, and attended various seminars and meetings. After a month, I went back to Erzebet and told her what a beautiful place Australia was. A few months later I got an offer to coach there, so off we went. I really enjoyed my time there, even meeting up with a few old Hungarian players who were out there, lads from Ferencvaros and MTK. It was a beautiful place; the weather was great, we had a lovely house and I enjoyed the scenery, gorgeous beaches, everything. The team wasn't bad and we did a lot of travelling – usually by plane in that massive country – playing in every city except Perth.

I came home at last to Budapest in 1991. But that's a story all of its own.

Afterword

Coming Home: The Return of the Exile

'At Kispest, one of the floodlights now stands where my living room once was.'

When Puskas left Hungary after the Uprising in 1956, he had absolutely no idea when, if ever, he would return to his homeland, where once he had been such a national hero. But towards the end of 1980, plans began to be laid in Hungary that would lead initially to his first visit, and eventually to his return to live in Budapest once again.

The first return to Hungary

The authorities in Hungary decided to back a project to make a filmed record of the Golden Squad's achievements, which would also include extended interviews with the surviving players. In 1981, it would be a quarter of a century since that unparalleled run of six years with only one defeat came to an end, and the film would celebrate the anniversary. But what would it be worth without a contribution from the greatest Hungarian player of all time: the captain of the Golden Squad himself?

Puskas: When I left Hungary and received the FA and FIFA ban, I swore to myself that I would never return. I felt bitter at such treatment, after so many years of giving my best for the nation. But after twenty-five years away, I did go home.

My wife played a major part in persuading me to return to help make the film, *The Golden Squad*. 'Uncle' Guszti Sebes arrived in Madrid too, where I was on holiday from the Egyptian job, to add his influence. I don't think I would have returned if they hadn't pushed me so hard. I had been approached by the people making the documentary and I had refused point blank. I'm not normally so stubborn, but I felt very strongly that I didn't want to go back to Budapest. Anyway, in the end I bowed to the pressure. Sebes and I flew to Paris *[probably to see Liverpool v Real in the European Cup Final on 27 May]*, where we met up with Szepesi. We travelled from there, on to Budapest. The reception at the airport took me completely by surprise.

Szepesi: In 1981, I was chairman of the Hungarian FA and I very much wanted Puskas to come home for the anniversary. Of course, the matter had to be raised at a senior political level, where it was agreed that the forthcoming match against England in Budapest *[a World Cup qualifier for Spain '82]* would be an appropriate occasion. I asked Sebes to go to Madrid and travel with Puskas from there to Paris to meet up with me.

On the plane from Paris to Budapest, Sebes sat next to Ocsi and I sat with Erzebet. She was quite uptight and told me that if anything went wrong she would personally do for me. But when we landed and she saw the crowd waiting to greet her husband, she relaxed. It was beautiful, a great day, a real celebration.

Puskas: When we arrived at the airport, it was packed with people who gave me the most moving and warm welcome I could have wished for. It was unbelievable; there were people screaming and shouting as if a pop star had arrived. Everyone wanted to embrace me, and there were faces of old friends everywhere that I could see as I was swept past them to get me in. I couldn't possibly greet everyone and I felt worried that it would hurt people if I missed them out. As soon as I could, I got away from the crowd to visit the Kispest cemetery where the graves of my parents lay; I had never visited my mother's before. Over the next few days, things settled down a bit and I did the interview they needed for the film.

The 'Old Boys' game in Budapest, 1981

Puskas: Then came the match. It had been decided that an 'Old Boys' game, Budapest v The Rest, would be played as an opening attraction before the Hungary v England World Cup qualifier *[on the evening of 6 June 1981]* at the Nepstadion *[England won 3–1]*. They had gathered as many of the Golden Squad together as possible and there were 65,000 in the stadium to watch the 'Old Boys' match – and this was at a time when attendances in Hungary had dropped catastrophically, even for international matches. It was an incredible night.

Tichy: I was in the changing-room before the match. It was bedlam. There were all sorts of people coming and going, shaking Puskas's hand, slapping backs and making jokes. He had such a big stomach that we couldn't find a shirt to fit him. Outside there was a huge crowd in the stadium and they hadn't come to watch the qualifying match.

Puskas: We had such a laugh in the changing-room before the match, myself, Buzanszky, Hidegkuti and others. We couldn't get the bloody kit on, we were so overweight, and we were dragging each other's shirts down over fat bellies. Many of the old team were still alive then, though some had gone, including of course Bozsik, and we thought much about those who could not be there. Absent friends.

The match itself was great fun – a 3–3 draw, I remember – and at the end we all lined up in the middle to thank the crowd and everybody. It was then that I stepped forward out of the line to face directly Janos Kadar and the political leaders who were ranged along the VIP balcony. I inclined my head towards them all. It was a gesture of respect. I felt it was the right thing to do because I had always feared coming back to anything less than a wholehearted welcome. I knew that without their consent the gathering at the airport and everything else would not have been possible. I was grateful that they had allowed me to come home in a proper way, and I felt at last that I had been forgiven for our failure to win the 1954 World Cup.

Again after the match, I was surrounded by people who wanted to shake my hand and congratulate me. I must have re-met every player I ever played with or against, and it was sometimes really difficult to remember them now, twenty-five years or more older than when we last met, but I smiled and nodded to everyone, anxious that no one should feel left out. It was a wonderful occasion; a great homecoming.

Afterwards

Puskas: After that visit in 1981, I felt able to return to Hungary on a regular basis. Whether I was working in Egypt, or later in Australia, I came back every summer for a few weeks and visited friends and relations, before going on to Spain for a holiday with my daughter's family. Some things in Budapest remained much the same, but of course others had altered considerably. Kispest, unfortunately, had been completely spoilt by new developments. Hundreds of small houses had been bulldozed to make room for a huge estate of high-rise blocks. The little 'town houses' with their small flats, where Bozsik and I had grown up together, were gone. They were so close to the Kispest stadium that one of the floodlights now stands where my living room once was. When I saw what had happened, a pain struck through my heart. We had spent so many good times here as kids, in places which no longer even existed.

I was coaching in Australia when Sebes died (31 January 1986). He was a very old man, in his mid 80s. Unfortunately, I was too far away to make it back to see him, but I have visited his grave many times since. I loved him very much. He was a good friend to my father, and he was like a father to me. Frankly, Hungarian football was finished as an international force after his death. It is true to say that during that post-war period in Hungary, there were a lot of very good players from which to forge a Golden Squad, but it was Sebes – with that fantastic energy and belief of his – who picked us and made us into a world-class side.

There were quite a few Hungarians in Australia and some of them began to talk to me about going home for good. After the collapse of communism, some of the leaders of the Democratic Forum which formed the newly elected government visited Australia and urged me to come home. They were saying that I could help the forlorn state of Hungarian football. It was interesting because this was a new generation of politicians; none of them knew me personally, yet I could feel how important it was for them to get me to return to Budapest. I refused at first, but after a few years I decided to go.

I was used to people in the football world wanting me back. When I was in Budapest for my few weeks every summer, people were always asking me to take on one football job or another. I had some major arguments about it. People at Honved wanted me to take over as coach, but I told them I was getting too old for the hassle. I was getting to the point where I wanted a break from football, at least from being up front and responsible for everything.

National coach

In 1992, Puskas returned to live in Budapest. He had hardly arrived (and was still living out of a hotel) when he was asked to become 'caretaker' coach of the national team until the permanent position could be filled, following the sudden resignation of Imre Jenei. Hungarian football was in a parlous state; Puskas didn't really want the job, even on a temporary basis, but he felt obliged to help out. Under his guidance the team did not prosper, losing to Sweden, Russia and, crucially, at home to little Iceland in a World Cup qualifier.

Puskas: I did it only for three months because there were a few important matches coming up and the coach had suddenly resigned. I insisted that it was only temporary. I think I could have been anything I wanted, they were so desperate, even chairman of the Hungarian FA but I didn't fancy that one bit. I love football, but you can keep the politics of it all. I just felt I had to help and I was glad when it was over.

Afterwards, I had long discussions with the FA officials about what kind of useful role I could play in the national set-up. Eventually they persuaded me to advise and assist them in international affairs, and to direct the youth coaching. It means that I do some travelling and receiving of foreign delegations – general handshaking duties – but the work with youngsters is enjoyable. I travel with the youth team. I keep busy and help where I can, but I find it hard to talk to modern Hungarian coaches; we don't speak the same language any more. I find their attitudes strange: they talk when they should listen, yet have nothing of importance to say when they do speak. But apparently that's normal in Hungary these days, and I'll just have to learn to get used to it. I do hope that things will improve for Hungarian football. We need money to spend on the development of a proper youth training policy, and I'll do my best to persuade commercial sponsors to provide it. That's the way it is these days.

At home

Today, Puskas and his wife Erzebet live comfortably in a modern apartment, not far from Moscow Square in Buda. When he walks the streets, sometimes the traffic stops, as people approach to shake the hand of the most famous Hungarian in the world, or shout 'Ocsi!' from their cars. Close to one of the Danube bridges in Budapest there is a bar called, simply, '6–3', and all over Hungary, for a while, a massive poster campaign advertised beer with a picture of Puskas and the headline: 'World-class!' Slowly, the city is getting used to having its greatest footballing hero home at last.

Puskas often meets up with the surviving members of the Golden Squad: Grosics and his reserve Geller, Buzanszky, Hidegkuti and Czibor (who has returned from Spain to live in Komarom). There are frequent anniversaries and footballing occasions where they regularly gather; old men now, easy in each other's company, with shared memories of some of the finest moments in football's living history.

Puskas looks well, though the expanse of his stomach – which he sometimes calls his 'company' – has kept pace with his increasing years. When he sits relaxed, he pulls up the legs of his trousers to keep cool, revealing feet so small they might almost belong to a boy; that left foot relaxed, yet – at least to an Englishman – still somehow fascinatingly menacing. He remains energetic, often travelling the world to lend his name to an event or appear in some television programme. In 1996, the Korean committee co-ordinating their successful bid for the 2002 World Cup asked him, as their guest, to remind everyone that he was the first captain to greet the first Korean in their first World Cup of 1954.

Puskas's apartment is not strewn with memorabilia of the many victories in his career. A casual visitor would not instantly realize it was the home of a great footballer. (One imagines that his life's belongings trail after him still, trying to catch up with the years of wandering.) Perhaps many of his medals and trophies remain in Spain with his daughter. But there are a few evidences, in his study, of the impact of his life, and not only on the world of football. One of them is a cup presented to him by representatives of Budapest's journalists, which reads:

To 'Ocsi' Puskas, International Football's most Prolific Goal-scorer. The 'kid brother' of the Nation.

Puskas is, in effect, a national monument.

Puskas: Hungary can be a difficult place, but I'm glad I've returned to the city of my birth and I think I will spend the rest of my days here now. I still like to get away to Spain to see my daughter Aniko, who now has two grown-up daughters of her own, and it's especially nice to miss out a few weeks of winter in Hungary. I don't think I have a great deal of time left in my current job but I'll do what I can for as long as I can, and then I'll say, Goodbye. I love the involvement with youngsters and I love my family, and this is enough for me.

As I look back, I see my life has had a single thread – just football – running right through it. It has been simple, direct, with no conflicting ambitions. From that moment as a little kid when I first heard the mysterious roar of the crowd in the Kispest stadium just a few metres away from our kitchen window, I suppose I was already spoken for.

In the end, God willing, I will be just an old man who loves football.

Sources

All contributions from Ferenc Puskas are taken from live interviews between 1993–96, in Budapest.

Other live interviews (1993–96)

Many of the quotes from the following are extracts taken from research interviews for the BBC TV series *Kicking and Screaming* are indicated in the text: (K&S)

Allison, Malcolm: English footballer and club manager
Barcs, Sandor: vice-president and president of the Hungarian FA
Buzanszky, Jeno: footballer in the Golden Squad
Czibor, Zoltan: footballer in the Golden Squad
Finney, Tom: England footballer
Grosics, Gyula: footballer in the Golden Squad
Haynes, Johnny: England footballer
Hidegkuti, Nandor: footballer in the Golden Squad
Matthews, Stanley: England footballer

Owen, Syd: England footballer
Szepesi, Gyorgy: leading Hungarian radio commentator and FA chairman
Taylor, Brian: of Bankfield House Community Centre, Liverpool
Tichy, Lajos: footballer for Budapest Locomotiv, Honved and Hungary
Vandor, Kalman: Hungarian sports journalist
Wright, Billy: captain of England
Winterbottom, Walter: England manager

The quotation from **Jim Baxter**, the Scotland footballer, is taken from the BBC radio series, *Great Scots*.

Hungarian sources

Bocsak, Miklos, 1983, *Kocsis es Czibor*, Sport, Budapest. This book is the source for all quotations of Budai, and those of Czibor inside quotation marks.

Grosics, Gyula, 1963, *Igy lattam a Kapubol*, (*'My View from the Goal'*), Sport, Budapest.

Hamori, Tibor, 1982, *Puskas, Legenda es Valosag* (*'Legend and Reality'*), Budapest. This book is the source for all quotations of Osterreicher.

Hidegkuti, Nandor and Fekete, Pal, 1965, *Obudatol Firenzeig* (*'From Old Buda to Florence'*), Sport, Budapest.

Ko, Andras, 1979, *Bozsik*, Sport, Budapest.

Sebes, Gusztav, 1981, *Oromok es Csalodasok* (*'Happiness and Disappointment'*), Gondolat, Budapest. This book is the source for all quotations of Sebes, with the permission of Erzebet Sebes.

Zsolt, Robert, 1989, *Puskas Ocsi*, Budapest.

English sources

Ellis, Arthur, 1962, *The Final Whistle*, London.
Finney, Tom, 1960, *Finney on Football*, The Sportsman's Book Club, London.
Glanville, Brian, 1973, *History of the World Cup*, London.
Green, Geoffrey, 1974, *Soccer in the Fifties*, London.
Griffiths, Mervyn, 1958, *The Man in the Middle*, London.
Johnston, Harry, 1954, *The Rocky Road to Wembley*, London.
Liddell, Billy, 1960, *My Soccer Story*, London.
Merrick, Gil, 1954, *I See It All*, London.
Miller, David, 1981, *Cup Magic*, London.
Widdows, Richard, 1973, *The Sixty Memorable Matches*, London.

Background historical sources in English

Lomax, Bill, 1976, *Hungary, 1956*, London.
Lomax, Bill (ed.), 1980, *Eyewitness in Hungary: the Soviet Invasion of 1956*, Nottingham.
Swain, Nigel, 1992, *Hungary: The Rise and Fall of Feasible Socialism*, London.